If you are searching for ways to energize or reenergize your spiritual journey, there are a couple of folks I want you to meet. Rick and Cindy Mercer have a story to tell that is true, candid, and at times raw. They describe their jagged journey and the power they didn't know existed that got them through it. You will find both hope and helpful tools as you walk beside two young people who were very lost but who ended up very found. If you or someone you love needs to discover how to have a transformational journey over a road that isn't always smooth, you'll find courage here. The narrative is well told and when you finish it, you just may be singing "He's All I Need."

Ruthie Jacobsen
Prayer Ministries director, retired
North American Division

Cindy Mercer has written a wonderful testimony of tragedy and ultimate redemption by the miraculous and steady work of God. Many will probably relate to aspects of this story and long to have the tangible delivery she and her husband experienced. If you read this book, your faith in God will increase. If you meditate on its lessons, you will experience a growing desire for more of God in your life. If you embrace the message of this book, your prayer life will change.

Ron E. M. Clouzet, DMin
Ministerial Association secretary
North Asian-Pacific Division

The message of this book issues forth from a heart that sheds personal tears in the night but exudes the joy of the Lord in the morning. It skillfully interweaves the inspirational and the transformational aspects of life's setbacks and comebacks. It is indeed a recommended read for those who desire to experience the God who is eager to do more abundantly than one can imagine.

Dr. Philip Samaan
Southern Adventist University,
School of Religion, professor

This is a gripping and transparent story of a young woman's journey of hope, failure, growth, and healing in the midst of seemingly insurmountable odds. Cindy dots her account with the "personalized," magnificent scriptural promises that were foundational for her tenacious journey and gives credit to her friends and family from various faith communities who supported and nurtured her. For Rick to give permission for the release of this story is a testimony to his spiritual depth and his commitment to helping others facing such challenges. Having known Cindy and Rick Mercer for almost a decade, I can truly say that is an extraordinary experience to have them wrap you in their peace and joy-filled intercessory embrace. You sense that God is close.

Donna Jackson
associate director, Spouses Ministerial leader
North American Division Ministerial Association

Cindy Mercer had to be totally engulfed in God's anointing to meticulously share her family's incredible journey with God. *Pray Big* defines the essence of intercessory prayer while at the same time capturing God's plan for those whom He calls. This book gave me far beyond what I was expecting. If there is anyone who doubts God hears and answers their prayers or doubts God's plan for their life, I strongly recommend reading and sharing this masterpiece of a story.

James Black
Prayer Ministries director
North American Division

Cindy shares a fascinating story about real life and real answers that help connect us to God. She wrestles honestly with hard questions about prayer, forgiveness, and deliverance. She shows us the power of grace to meet our doubts and pain and the transforming prayer that flows when we surrender to God the dreams of our hearts to do whatever He wills. I know firsthand the blessing of Rick and Cindy Mercer's friendship and ministry. They bring practical hope in the promises of God.

Kelly Mowrer
Live at the Well Ministries founder

PRAY BIG

GOD CAN DO
SO MUCH MORE!

CINDY MERCER

Pacific Press®
Publishing Association
Nampa, Idaho | www.pacificpress.com

Cover design by Rebecca Carpenter
Cover photograph by Luke Davis | MainStreet Studios, Siloam Springs, Arkansas
Inside design by Aaron Troia

You can obtain additional copies of this book by calling toll-free 1-800-765-6955 or by visiting
http://www.adventistbookcenter.com.

Library of Congress Cataloging-in-Publication Data

Names: Mercer, Cindy (Pastor's wife), author.
Title: Pray big / Cindy Mercer.
Description: Nampa, Idaho : Pacific Press Publishing Association, [2020] | Summary: "A story
    about the transforming power of prayer in the life of the Mercer family"— Provided by
    publisher.
Identifiers: LCCN 2019059726 | ISBN 9780816366484 (paperback) | ISBN 9780816366491
    (kindle edition)
Subjects: LCSH: Spouses of clergy—Religious life. | Christian women—Religious life. |
    Mercer, Cindy (Pastor's wife) | Prayer—Christianity.
Classification: LCC BV4395 .M465 2020 | DDC 277.308/3092 [B]—dc23
LC record available at https://lccn.loc.gov/2019059726

February 2020

Dedication

First and foremost, I dedicate this memoir of faith and prayer journey to the Author and Finisher of my faith—Jesus Christ. You are my everything!

This book is also dedicated to every reader who will take God at His Word and truly believe that He will and can do everything He says He will do.

Contents

Foreword

Our Lord is the great Miracle Worker! He is the Stronghold Breaker! Yet all over the world we see precious individuals, families, and churches struggling with discouragement because the enemy sets up oppressive obstacles. Everything looks impossible—until God steps in and barriers start to fall. One of our deepest joys is to hear these stories of His deliverance and grace! We stand amazed as He transforms despair into hope, defeat into explosive adventures of growth in Him!

The lives and ministry of Rick and Cindy Mercer are one of His best stories! Our friendship with them over the years has touched and changed our lives. We've also seen the impact of their testimony on thousands of others.

Cindy's difficult spiritual journey broke through into flourishing leadership gifts for prayer ministries, women's ministries and a multitude of speaking and teaching opportunities. Rick's miraculous call into pastoral ministry now grows and thrives in multiple venues as he willingly shares the testimony of his past addictions and God's power to save us all. Whether speaking individually or together, Rick and Cindy bring hope through their openness and vulnerability. They know the challenges and attacks faced by men, women, and marriages everywhere. They understand the temptation to despair about relationships, sins, and unbelievably hard situations—to pray and try to overcome but without seeing results. They know how it feels to almost give up. But they also know the truth of these words from Ellen White that we love, "There is no danger that the Lord will neglect the prayers of His people. The danger is that in temptation and trial they will become discouraged, and fail to persevere in prayer."[1]

The testimony shared in this book relates to every one of us. We may not be struggling with obvious addictions and sins, but we all need transformation! We all seek real conversation with Jesus in prayer! We all long for the continued life-changing presence of His Spirit—and to see His work in our hearts impact those around us who also struggle.

Janet felt so moved by Cindy's testimony that she strongly encouraged her to put it in the form of this book. Now you can experience God's abundant blessing of that prayerful effort for yourself!

The wonderful endorsements accompanying this book underscore the value of its message. They come from fellow Christians we profoundly respect because their walk with Jesus is real. We add our whole-hearted agreement to their beautiful words.

Just now, God is at work intensely in these last days! The Holy Spirit is preparing the final, great breakthroughs before Jesus returns very soon!

We encourage you to read this story of deliverance and then help spread the blessing. Share this book widely with others who need a life change too! God always gives so much more than we could ever ask or dream!

We know He will use this powerful testimony from Rick and Cindy to bring hope, courage, perseverance, faith, and freedom.

Jerry and Janet Page
secretary and associate secretary
General Conference Ministerial Association

---

1. Ellen G. White, *Christ's Object Lessons* (Washington, DC: Review and Herald®, 1941), 175.

Author's Preface

As you read this narrative journey involving joy, suspense, laughter, tears, confusion, and pain, please keep in mind—it's *my* personal testimony. Several accounts in the following pages are conversations between me and God, which I've interpreted to be His voice giving *me* direction moment by moment. In addition, it is not my purpose to advise you on the physical or medical aspect of fasting. *Pray Big* is written from a spiritual perspective and is based on my personal experience. To the best of my ability, I have used multiple journal entries and memories and to weave a story that I'm praying will leave you with hope and assurance for your individual situation. To protect and provide respect, names and places have been omitted or changed when necessary. I'm praying by the end of the book, you *will* discover God *is* able to do exceedingly, abundantly more, so much more, than you could ever think or imagine!

Great is His faithfulness!

Introduction

Have you ever asked God for something more, not knowing for sure what you might get in return?

I have shared the following testimony for over twelve years around the world and found that people sometimes experience a bit of shock when they hear it. A few of them are so startled they're not sure they should keep listening.

But because I'm a pastor's wife (and still married to the husband of my story), people are usually willing to set aside their surprise to learn how God stepped into the nightmare of our marriage and led me to hope, through prayer, that changed everything!

If you long for God's favor, but sometimes find it elusive or unattainable, this book is for you.

It is also for people who are tired of trying to use just the right words when they pray—only to hear silence from God.

And it's for anyone who knows all the correct church etiquette but still feels stale—those who sometimes hear a little voice in their hearts whispering, *There has to be something more.*

Growing up, my prayers consisted of mainly small talk with God. My words were spiritually polite and carefully scripted.

Even though I spoke to Him occasionally throughout my day, I kept my expectations low because it seemed safer that way. Secretly, I felt almost hypocritical. I never dared to pray for anything truly important because, deep down, I didn't believe He would answer.

Deep down, I wanted more. I wanted something real, something different.

Eventually, I embarked on a journey with God lasting longer than I ever imagined, and it looked nothing like what I expected. I also discovered that prayer doesn't always turn out tidy and precise—but His answers fill us with awe.

This book is about hope. This book is about new beginnings. This book is about miracles—and so much more!

Now to Him who is able to do exceedingly abundantly
above all that we ask or think,
according to the power that works in us,
to Him be glory in the church by Christ Jesus
to all generations, forever and ever.
Amen.

—Ephesians 3:20, 21

Chapter 1

March 19, 1997

My day started with a small, half-hearted prayer and low expectations. It felt safe that way—certainly less room for disappointment if things didn't work out.

I had already learned life sometimes threw painful, unexpected curveballs that destroyed dreams. Some dreams shattered so completely that all of my church activities, Bible-study groups, good intentions, and hard work couldn't put them back together again.

I longed for God's favor in my life. But it felt elusive.

And even if I ever *really* found it, I still knew some of my idyllic life plans were gone forever.

I was a proper Southern girl—with proper Southern dreams. My grand life story—first designed when my young heart brimmed with confidence and hope—held four vital pieces:

1. I would be a valued employee in a respected job.
2. I would be an outstanding wife—a cheerleader and support to my successful husband who would lavishly return my devotion.
3. I would be that "best mom ever," showering love over my adoring children.

4. We would all sit together in church—the polished, perfect family. My husband would gently hold my hand or put his arm around me as we received our weekly experience of God. Then we'd head home to go four-wheelin' or fishing or to ride horses.

Of course, during the week, we'd all drive back to church (in our Suburban) to attend small-group Bible studies and youth activities. My grand life story included *plenty* of God activities scheduled into *all* the suitable places.

I grew up playing along the Red River in a remote corner of southwest Arkansas surrounded by lush fields of corn, soybeans, and wheat. Bald eagles soared overhead and built nests in the fragrant loblolly pines spearing up along the banks. For 130 years, my ancestors owned and operated the Spring Bank Ferry, carrying the sparse traffic of State Highway 160 on the five-minute crossing from bank to bank.

On hot summer days, my adored older brother Rodney and I would ride our bikes down the slope, out across the ramp, and onto the bright orange wooden ferry. My dad, who passed the stringent Coast Guard test on his first try, would pilot us over to a sandbar where we could safely play. We would run around, swim, and build sandcastles until he got off work.

Then he'd load our bikes into the back of his truck and drive us home to eat one of Momma's delicious meals. There would be plenty of sweet tea or grape Kool-Aid and a homemade blackberry cobbler, made with blackberries freshly picked along our country road.

My grand life story included a chapter that looked just exactly like this—the perfect loving family.

One day I realized the chapter wasn't there anymore and never would be again.

Like the Red River snaking south, my life wound in and out of two failed marriages. I first married at the young age of eighteen, only to divorce four years later. After less than a year, I married again, and that marriage also ended with a jarring break and lingering pain.

Whole chapters of my beautiful dream were now forever deleted. There would be no husband sitting lovingly beside me in church. I wouldn't be a wonderful wife encouraging my successful man or building a home and a future.

My shiny hopes faded to bitter disappointment—a dull aching regret. I still sheepishly went to church most weeks, but I sat alone—feeling like everyone else knew how miserable I was.

Yet there was one bright blessing of joy and purpose in my life—my precious two-year-old son Tyler, born during my second marriage. I vowed to support and care for him. I would dig in and build something strong and worthwhile for Tyler and me.

By now, I was twenty-six years old and working as a surgical nurse at Jefferson Regional Medical Center in Pine Bluff, Arkansas. That first piece of my dream, at least, was still intact. I thought I might go back to school and continue my education, but I felt uncertain about the best way to juggle everything. I considered moving back to live near my parents.

But first, I needed to get through the looming evening of March 19, 1997. I felt a mix of anticipation and dread and couldn't believe I'd gotten caught up in something so ridiculous.

A few weeks earlier, I'd gone for my normal appointment at Rumors Hair Salon. I had known Donna, my stylist, for about a year and enjoyed her thoughtfulness and sense of humor. But that day, I learned she had quite the agenda prepared for me.

She didn't waste any time launching forth as she began to section and cut my hair.

"So, you don't have a boyfriend, do you, Cindy?" *Snip, snip, snip.*

Sensing potential quicksand, I replied quickly, "Hmm, not exactly. I'm actually making plans to move back where my parents live." (My plans grew firmer by the minute.)

Snip, snip, snip. "Well, the process of moving could take a little while, couldn't it? Wouldn't you like to meet someone in the meantime?"

"Uh . . ."

"Girl, I'd love for you to meet my brother Rick! He's just the best! I know I'm probably a bit biased, but he's such a great guy. He deserves someone as nice as you in his life."

I wondered if I should bolt and finish cutting my hair at home. But Donna was just getting warmed up.

"He's been divorced about five years now, but he's on really good terms with his ex. They even share joint custody. His boys are precious as all get-out—Brooks is six, and Farron is seven."

Snip, snip, snip.

Donna rolled on. "Did I mention that Rick's a CPA? He actually has two offices! His clients just adore him! One office is in town, and the other is out at his farm. Girl, you should see that farm he's got going. He contracts with a nationwide poultry industry and has lots of people working for him. Rick's a go-getter for sure!"

Clearly, Donna thought her brother hung the moon. And the more she shared, the more I felt a tiny ribbon flame of interest begin to spark and flicker deep inside. Rick Mercer sounded quite intriguing.

As I handed Donna the check for her services, I told her I would *think* about meeting him and *perhaps* be in touch with her.

"That's great, girl! Don't wait too long," she grinned.

As busy as I was, I couldn't stop thinking about the possibility of meeting someone as genuinely nice as Donna's brother sounded. The days flew by as I mulled it over.

My curiosity took a giant leap forward when *two* other friends separately approached me about a great guy they wanted me to meet—a real pillar of the community named Rick Mercer.

After the third independent endorsement, I finally caved in and called Donna for his number. *A real friend would sure feel good in my life about now,* I reasoned. *I would hate to miss out on a golden opportunity.*

That night, I sat in my little living room with butterflies in my stomach as I dialed the phone number. *This is going to be just another mistake in my stellar collection,* I told myself. *Don't get your hopes up.*

"Hello." I jumped a little when Rick answered.

"Hi, Rick," I answered, trying to sound casual, "this is Cindy—Donna's friend."

"Hi, Cindy! I'm not sure how she talked you into this, but thanks for taking the time."

I couldn't believe how easy Rick was to talk with—his deep, warm, kind voice and genuine interest flowed over my wounded, aching heart. My little flame of hope fanned a bit higher.

We discovered lots of shared family values. He told me about coaching his son's ball team and building forts with his boys. *He is a devoted dad,* I thought approvingly.

God Can Do So Much More

We exchanged the glossy version of our life stories—none of the dirty laundry at this point, of course.

After Rick graduated high school, he worked offshore in the Gulf of Mexico, making big money with his merchant marine license. (I already knew, courtesy of Donna, that he drove both a Porsche and a Jaguar.) Once the oil crunch hit, he went to college, flew through with a straight 4.0 grade point average, and aced his certified public accountant exam in one pass.

He came back home and bought a house with fifteen acres. His CPA business now served four hundred clients spread between the two offices. And his thriving commercial poultry operation, with four large poultry houses, was on track for expansion.

I already knew his family was highly respected in the area—now, I found myself enamored with his goals and aspirations. *Two separate businesses with employees*, I marveled. *You don't build that kind of setup unless you're responsible.*

Against all the odds, it was beginning to feel like I'd hit the jackpot. But even though Rick sounded like quite a catch, I proceeded cautiously, moving along to my list of potential deal-breaking questions:

Do you believe in God? (Of course.)
Do you smoke or do drugs? (No.)
Do you drink? (Only socially.)

Drinking alcohol was completely acceptable to me because everyone I knew consumed alcohol occasionally. I had grown up with my parents hosting what we called "play days." Daddy was a professional calf-roper for fifteen years, and we had a roping arena at our home. People would come from all over, bringing their horses to practice roping cattle or to enjoy riding in the arena. We would set up tables under the trees and grill burgers while everyone talked and laughed and music played. Momma always made her famous chocolate pies.

Most all the adults drank alcohol at play days, except Momma. Sometimes, after several hours of drinking, things might morph and become a bit tense. Someone might start cussin' or spoiling for a fight, and Daddy would have to run him off. Or maybe sometimes I noticed my parents might argue a bit more after Daddy drank for an evening, but come next morning, everything was fine again.

Social drinking was normal—*everybody* did it. I didn't see any red flags there.

Pray Big

Before the conversation was over, Rick asked if we could meet face-to-face. I still felt a little wary, but my flame of hope was burning too strongly to turn back now. Was he too good to be true? There was only one way to find out.

I agreed to meet him on March 19. There. It was settled—my first official blind date.

In the days that followed, panic set in. *Eeeeek! What was I thinking? I should just back out now.* A million excuses began running through my mind.

The big question looping repeatedly was, *Have you really stooped to this kind of desperation, Cindy? What if he looks like a squat green toad—or an ax murderer?*

The evening finally came, and I opened the door slowly. My first glance left me pleasantly relieved. My dreaded "squat green toad" looked more like Prince Charming with gorgeous green eyes wearing an L. L. Bean sweater.

"Are you Rick?" I asked hesitantly.

"Yes," he answered smiling.

The moment felt strangely awkward. *What do you expect from a blind date, Cindy?*

But the awkwardness quickly disappeared. And the more we talked, the more I noticed something else disappearing. The crushing sense of hopelessness and failure settled so heavily in my heart now began lifting and vanishing like the early morning mist over the Red River.

Talking and laughing easily, we went to Bonanza for dinner. But the food didn't matter. We were lost in captivating discovery.

Our conversation ran deep—focused on family and future dreams. We also talked a lot about God.

Rick grew up attending the Methodist church, where his mom was a matriarch and pillar of support. "I got a pin for faithful attendance," he told me, "because my mom took me to church for so many years in a row."

"My momma was the same way," I smiled. "We went to Mount Zion Baptist Church every Sunday. Pastor Allen Hoven always made an altar call. When I was twelve, I made my pilgrimage to the front. I felt God sort of pull me out of the seat and draw me down the aisle. Pastor Hoven asked if I wanted to give my life to the Lord, and I said yes."

I described for Rick how special I felt on the day I was baptized. We didn't have robes—I just wore a little red-striped T-shirt and my blue jeans. But I never forgot going down into the water in that beautiful, simple ceremony. The church gave me a small, red Bible that I treasured always.

Rick shared his private, unusual commitment to God too.

"You know how people make a wish when they see a shooting star?" he asked. "Well, for as many years back as I can remember, whenever I see a shooting star, my wish is that I could give my whole heart to God. I don't think I've figured out how to do it quite right yet, but I know I want to."

My heart flooded with joy. Our lives were poised and responsive for more of Jesus! Hope was now fully alive, and I knew I was part of a miracle.

My grand life story was being resurrected from the ashes in front of my eyes.

Only God could bring a new life like this. Only God could drop the missing piece of my puzzle right into my lap so unexpectedly.

But as the evening wrapped up and we returned to my house, I felt the old nagging doubts and awkwardness slinking back. *Should I ask him in? What if he doesn't feel anything at all like I do? What if he only intends to say good night and never see me again?*

I fumbled out, "Would you like to come in for a bit?"

I needn't have worried. Our easy conversation quickly returned as we sat side by side on my blue-and-whited striped sofa. I was pretty sure he was about to ask me for another date.

But instead, Rick looked deep into my eyes and spoke with a very soft and determined voice.

"Cindy, you're what I've been looking for—and you're all I need. We've talked about giving our lives to God and serving Him. I meant it, and you meant it, and I believe God knows we mean it.

"Cindy, will you marry me?"

I didn't even hesitate.

As soon as Rick left, I ran and jumped on my bed like a teenager! Without even looking at the time, I called my close friend Kristi. She had been anxiously waiting for all the details of the evening. Not realizing it was two in the morning, I bubbled and gushed out a moment-by-moment recall of the night's events. She couldn't believe how well everything had gone. I couldn't contain my excitement any longer. She about passed out as I informed her I was going to marry my blind date, Rick Mercer!

That night I started a brand-new journal.

Pray Big

March 19, 1997

Tonight I met the love of my life, the one I want to love, take care of, laugh and cry with, and grow old with.

Dear Lord, You are so good to Rick and me. We prayed about this, and we know this is Your will and the right plan for us. We both know without a shadow of a doubt that we are going to spend the rest of our lives together.

Thank You, God, for sending him to me, and I promise You we will serve You. You have blessed us far more than we could believe.

My grand life story was back on track and better than ever! The journey ahead felt full of promise and hope.

Maybe some people would wonder how in the world I could say yes to a marriage proposal on a blind first date. But they'd understand eventually—after they saw the beautiful life we would build together.

I overflowed with confidence that everything I'd discovered about Rick contained all the essential pieces for my grand life dream. I believed with all my heart that God was providing an incredible answer to my longing for *something more*, and I wasn't going to miss it.

I was off to the promised land with Rick Mercer!

But I didn't realize how quickly things could change.

I didn't know God was about to show me that my grand life story was far too small for the Author of the universe.

I had no idea He was about to transform the *ordinary* pieces of my dream with an *exceedingly abundant* story only He could write.

And I had no idea God's grand life story for Cindy looked radically different than *all* my prayers—or that each piece of my dream would shatter into a million shards before I would see His.

Chapter 2

Spring drifts into Arkansas with masses of yellow jonquils and clouds of magnolia blossoms. I felt perfectly in tune with this dazzling season of new life as I floated into work the next morning.

Breezing around with a glowing smile, I beamed my good news to one and all.

"I've never met such a gentleman in my life," I raved to one group.

"He's such a fantastic family man," I gushed to another.

My friends and coworkers rejoiced with me as I dispensed giddy descriptions of the amazing Rick Mercer. Many of them remarked they hadn't seen me this happy in a very long time.

With the initial flurry of announcements completed, I settled down at my desk near the glass-front doors. Just before lunch, a florist van arrived to deliver an extravagant bouquet of red roses.

The card read, "Today is the first day of the rest of our lives."

My heart soared higher. Our status was officially confirmed and secure! Cloud nine was my current location, and I was *never* coming down!

Rick lived about thirty minutes south of my home, and most fortuitously, I had a patient visit scheduled near Rick's farm that same night. During weeknights, I helped a home-health agency, which supplemented my income from my job at the surgery center.

I giddily phoned Rick to thank him for the beautiful flowers and message. During our conversation, I mentioned I'd be in his area later.

"Why don't you come for supper and bring Tyler to meet the boys," he invited.

"That sounds wonderful," I eagerly accepted, "but please don't go to any trouble."

"Don't worry about that," he laughed, "I know what kids like. My boys think I'm a terrific chef!"

I soon discovered a favorite tradition before meals involved Rick teasingly asking Brooks and Farron, "Who's the best cook in the whole wide world?"

"Daddy!" they'd yell happily, as he opened a can of Campbell's SpaghettiOs with fanfare and flourish. Of course, he had the standard repertoire of hot dogs and burgers in regular rotation as well.

We kept the meal kid-friendly that night and planned a proper date for the next evening.

"We'll stop by and say hi to my folks first," Rick said. "They can't wait to meet you!" I felt a flicker of nerves and hoped I'd make a good impression.

Meanwhile, Rick's boys certainly made a *fine* impression with me. They adored their fun-loving dad, who often played with them but also required obedience and good manners. All of my questions were answered with a polite "Yes, ma'am" or "No, ma'am."

And they were wonderfully patient with little Tyler. Shortly after we arrived, they asked, "Miss Cindy, could we please take Tyler to show him our toys?" and my heart melted further into bliss.

March 20, 1997

I cannot wipe this smile off my face. Rick Mercer has made me a new woman. I love him so much and deeper than I ever thought I would.

He is the kindest man I ever met. He's a breath of fresh air. Tonight, we listened to music and watched the kids play.

The next evening, I wore an elegant cream, satin blouse and black dress slacks for our date to The Village Steakhouse over in Star City. But first I would meet Rick's parents, Sam and Brenda.

I already knew they were *highly* esteemed in the community. Sam raised commercial poultry also and was known as a great employer for teenagers who needed weekend and summer work. Brenda had recently retired from her position as a nursing home administrator and was helping Rick at his home CPA office.

They were so friendly and welcoming.

"It's wonderful to meet you, hon," Brenda said, obliterating my nerves with her warm hug. Sam was easygoing and full of questions about my family. I basked in his obvious approval of our relationship. There was much laughter and teasing before we headed out.

The rest of the evening passed in a dream of candlelight and starlight. We enjoyed the delicious prime rib and deliberated over the wedding date. We needed to wait until tax season was over, plus I wanted a chance to pull together a few special touches for the friends and family who would gather.

I *knew* this marriage would go the distance, and I wanted our wedding day to be a festive celebration filled with wonderful memories.

We decided to be married at Rick's house on May 3. We borrowed folding chairs from his mom's church and asked her pastor, Brother Rusty, to marry us.

We also talked about our life beyond the wedding.

We discovered right away that we both held the dream of having a child together. I could already picture our three precious little boys welcoming their tiny new sibling with wide-eyed wonder.

Throughout the evening, I kept looking at Rick in awe. How amazing that this handsome, kind man was going to become my husband.

God, he is so wonderful! I prayed silently. *Please don't let him ever leave me.*

All at once, something seemed to shift uncomfortably in my heart. Deep down, beneath all the joy, I felt almost afraid. I had never prayed like this before—like there were real consequences at stake.

What did I actually know about God and how to talk to Him when it *really* mattered?

I was used to short, polite prayers, maybe an expression of thankfulness before holiday meals, sort of like reciting the Pledge of Allegiance on the Fourth of July. Maybe I'd present Him with some brief, wishful thought (*please help it not to rain tomorrow*) in case He wanted to sign off on it. Of course, if He didn't, it was no big deal—I'd just move on to plan B.

But now I felt almost anxious and urgent—I *wanted* this marriage to work!

I didn't *have* a plan B. But I also didn't know exactly how to tap into any Divine help that might give me an extra edge.

What should I say? How should I phrase it? Was I even holy enough to motivate God to answer me? I mean, I went to church a couple times a week—did that count? It had crossed my mind occasionally that maybe I should try reading my Bible in between those church visits, but I'd never acted on it. Was that going to be a negative mark against me now? How did prayer work when you really needed an answer?

I suddenly thought of my Papaw Vestal with his deep bass voice. When I was a little girl, we'd sit together on his wide porch that wrapped around their house. We would rock slowly in the heavy porch swing, savoring the aroma of Mamaw's chicken and dumplings simmering on the stove.

Papaw *loved* to sing. He taught me his favorite song, "Just a Little Talk With Jesus," while our feet pushed the swing back and forth in a lazy rhythm. His rich, strong voice started each line, and my little tremolo piped in as we'd sing. Sometimes I wondered how that "little talk with Jesus" made everything all right. Did it even exist outside of a song? I didn't know.[1]

My experience with God and church seemed so ordinary, so convenient and unremarkable—just another proper accessory to a proper life.

Even when I was young, though, I'd sometimes think, *There has to be something more than this.* I would vaguely wonder how I could uncover this deeper *knowledge* of God—a *real* connection that was *alive* and *profound*.

Almost always, I'd remember Tammy—my childhood best friend—and her mom, Ernestine (who everyone called Ernie). Tammy's dad was a pastor, and I deeply enjoyed going to church with them. Their genuine love of God and lively worship services filled my little seeking heart with amazement.

These people sure are holy, I'd muse.

I loved visiting their home too. Ms. Ernie was so welcoming and easy to talk with. One day I stood in their kitchen, my questions about God and life spilling out. It felt wonderfully comfortable to listen while Ms. Ernie patiently answered and shared her thoughts.

"Cindy," she said as we finished up, "you ask a lot of deep questions for a young girl. I know that God's got something special for your life!"

I never forgot that moment. I trusted her words.

Even if I don't have all the answers yet, I'd assure myself, *God has something special for my life.*

God Can Do So Much More

In the days ahead, Rick and I were inseparable, and our plans raced along. I introduced him to my trusted friend Kristi and felt especially delighted to receive her "go ahead" stamp of enthusiastic approval.

Almost every evening after work, I headed out to Rick's house. Things were somewhat torn up because he was remodeling, but I loved just sitting in the same room together while he slogged through the hectic tax season.

I also enjoyed watching him talk with clients. He took great care explaining business details and patiently answering their questions. He interacted smoothly with a wide variety of ages and income levels and always said just the right words.

Rick wanted to quickly introduce me to as many friends and family members as possible. He was crazy about me, and I was crazy about him—and we wanted *everyone* to know.

We made our rounds in the community and began hosting social gatherings at the house. Rick was an outstanding chef, and he often hosted crawfish boils, adding in all my favorites of fresh lemon halves, baby red potatoes, sweet corn on the cob, and plenty of Old Bay Seasoning.

Everyone sat around talking and laughing, digging into generous piles of this delicious goodness and washing it down with plenty of ice-cold beer. The kids ran around playing, and life simply couldn't be any better.

The future stretched out before us in a beautiful panorama. If only we could get past one *final* troublesome hurdle looming uncomfortably at hand.

Plain and simple, I was scared for Rick to meet my dad.

M. R. Duncan rigorously held himself, and everyone else, to the *strictest* standards. Widely known as an outstanding businessman, he was both hardworking and hardheaded in equal measure. Only a fool tried to pull a fast one on M. R.—or on anyone he loved. I knew his protectiveness of me had ratcheted into high gear. He didn't want me, or Tyler, hurt.

But Daddy also had a gorgeous smile and deep blue eyes. He laughed a lot and could talk the horns off of a billy goat. I fervently hoped that some of his famed affability would at least provide a cordial veneer for our first visit.

Of course, I'd been burning up the phone lines with Momma (my most trusted confidant), singing Rick's praises incessantly. I could just picture my dad once he found out we were coming.

"Well, it's about time we set eyes on him, Mary Ann!" he'd tell Momma. "I want to scope this guy out myself!"

"Now, M. R.," she'd answer firmly, "don't you go saying anything *strange* and making this complicated!"

That weekend, Rick and I loaded up the three boys and traveled south. I tried to calm my thoughts as the peaceful scenery flashed past.

Acres of pastures stretched out on either side of the road, wet and boggy during the winter—but dried now under the warm spring sun and filled with grazing cattle. The boys chattered and laughed in the back seat.

All too soon, we arrived, and I relaxed almost immediately. Rick won M. R.'s approval quickly, striking common ground with discussions of farming and livestock. Rick knew how to talk the lingo.

I caught Daddy's eye and could almost read his mind. *He's a farmer like us! This guy's going to take care of my little girl!*

While Tyler pulled out all his favorite toys and showed Brooks and Farron around, Momma dished up her homemade fried chicken and mashed potatoes.

"He's a responsible, hardworking man!" she told me approvingly.

I beamed as we all sat down to a perfect dinner finished with Momma's legendary peanut-butter-and-chocolate cake. Afterward, she pulled me aside.

"I really like him!" she pronounced. "You'd be *crazy* not to marry him!"

Our dash to the altar continued down the home stretch.

But a week before the wedding, we jounced into our first little pothole. Rick came to me with an unusual piece of news.

"You know Art, the guy helping me remodel the house? Well, his folks live in Savannah, so he's going to fly to Georgia with us when we go on our honeymoon."

What in the world?

I felt my face freeze.

I *certainly* hadn't planned to begin my honeymoon as a party of *three*. How could Rick even consider that?

"We'll just drive him to his parents' house," Rick said hastily. "We can drop him off and then be on our way."

My thoughts raced. This was no time for a scene. Besides, was it really all that big of a deal? Quickly, I fell into my comfort zone—stepping nimbly onto the path of least resistance. I was skilled and agile from long years of practice.

Just be flexible, Cindy! This means nothing in the grand scheme of things, I assured myself.

God Can Do So Much More

Donna did my hair on May 3, 1997. Six weeks after that first date she'd set in motion, my hairdresser became my sister-in-law.

Momma handed me the gorgeous bouquet she'd made with pink, cream, and yellow roses, and I walked out past the latticed breezeway covered with swags of ivy to stand beside the love of my life.

Surrounded by our dearest friends and family, Brother Rusty pronounced us husband and wife—Mr. and Mrs. Rick and Cindy Mercer—complete with a ready-made family of three adorable boys. The little merry band of brothers commenced eating cake as soon as we gave the green light!

I am certain that Brother Rusty said a prayer that day—maybe more than one. I don't remember. A blissful haze of hope and laughter, conversation, and well-wishes surrounded me.

God receded to the distant edges of my life without me even noticing.

During the past hectic weeks, my regular schedule had understandably fallen by the wayside. Planning a wedding and blending a family consumed my time and focus.

Activities such as church or aerobics class slid far down the ladder of priorities. God was, after all, just one of my weekly appointments—to be kept when convenient. Recently, my calendar had simply been too full.

However, I felt certain the situation was only temporary. *Of course*, I'd go to church again—once we returned from the honeymoon and life got back to normal.

I was about to discover that I would never see my old "normal" again. Like Joseph in Egypt, I was heading into seven years of ravaging famine—a barren wilderness where everything "normal" withered and perished.

But unlike Joseph, I never saw it coming.

---

1. Cleavant Derricks, "Just a Little Talk With Jesus," Stamps-Baxter, 1937.

Chapter 3

Early the next morning, Rick and I drove to the Little Rock airport to begin our honeymoon. We schlepped along Art, the carpenter, like an oversized piece of Samsonite. As far as I was concerned, we couldn't drop him off at his parents' house soon enough.

Of course, I kept my thoughts private and a pleasant smile firmly in place. Art was actually a very personable guy—I just didn't want him on my honeymoon, not even for a few hours. Nevertheless, here we were.

I kept giving myself little pep talks. *Just hang in there, Cindy—we're almost to Savannah. We'll be alone soon.*

Once we got our rental car, Rick asked me to drive so that he and Art could pick up some refreshments at a liquor store to enjoy on the way. This felt reasonable—there was nothing unusual about the guys sharing a relaxing drink after the flight. Plus, I looked forward to driving our snazzy rental—a sharp burgundy Chrysler Sebring convertible!

We put the top down, and the wind felt exhilarating as we zipped along. Rick and Art drank companionably while Art occasionally gave me directions.

"Right up there's the homeplace," he finally pointed. I pulled in with relief. *Thank goodness the end's in sight,* I rejoiced. I intended to make small talk with Art's parents and be on our way directly.

However, once we stepped inside, Art excused himself for a moment. He came back carrying a glass mason jar of real, sure enough, home-brewed, Georgia moonshine.

God Can Do So Much More

My eyes watered when he unscrewed the lid. I had never experienced white lightnin' before! Visions of Elliot Ness, Prohibition, speakeasies, and old copper stills deep in the woods flashed through my mind.

It struck me that Rick and Art seemed quite relaxed about it all—passing the jar back and forth like pros. But once the liquor hit their systems, the results were instantaneous.

I watched in disbelief as they went from zero to sixty in ten seconds. Their faces got bright red, and their laughter grew boisterously loud.

I was flabbergasted.

I had never seen Rick so beamed up and giddy. I had seen him drinking socially plenty of times, but I'd never witnessed *anything* like this!

Rick and Art sloshed the jar back and forth, laughing raucously, while time crept along for me. Obviously, we stayed much longer than I'd *ever* anticipated. I made polite conversation with Art's family until Rick was ready to leave.

Hours later, we finally drove away. I mulled over the events that had just taken place. Rick was still buzzing with high spirits, so the mood didn't exactly feel conducive for a heart-to-heart about romance and honeymoons and reasonable expectations.

Besides, I wasn't even sure what I'd say. I certainly didn't want to start anything uncomfortable.

It's all over now anyway, I reasoned, enjoying the warm sun on my face and the wind whipping through my hair.

Maybe Rick just felt a few jitters about being married again, and this was his way of working them out. After all, we're on our honeymoon, and he's had so many tax deadlines hanging over him. He probably just wanted to unwind.

All in all, it seemed best to let it go. I put it aside and looked forward to enjoying the days ahead.

The Savannah waterfront charmed us with its history—both old and new. There was the famous "Waving Girl" statue, and the new Olympic torch sculpture commemorating the yachting events held a year prior during the 1996 Summer Olympics.

But it was the historic architecture that fascinated us. Rick's dream was to continue the remodel of our home using old wooden doors and beams and filling it with antiques. We wandered hand and hand, often pausing to snap photos of the beautiful, old buildings with wonderful character.

We enjoyed a romantic riverboat cruise and ate meals in colorful cafés along the water. Lingering over delicious food, we'd discuss plans and build castles of dreams about our future.

After a few days, we headed on to Charleston and a lovely, little two-story condo. But another unsettling experience lay ahead.

I had been getting ready to go out while Rick waited downstairs. When I walked down to join him, I knew immediately he hadn't heard or seen me coming. He stood facing away from me but angled enough that I could see the cigarette he casually lit. He held it comfortably—I could tell this was no first-time occurrence or irregular habit.

I quickly stepped back out of sight. I didn't want him to see me, and I didn't know what to say. *How odd,* I thought. *I know he told me before our first date that he didn't smoke.* I didn't want to think of him *deceiving* me, but I couldn't come up with any easy explanation.

As usual, I said nothing and hoped this was somehow a temporary lapse.

But I was disturbed. I remembered the alarming transformation when he and Art drank the moonshine—how he turned into someone I didn't even recognize.

I returned home with more than a collection of special memories and fun photos. As much as I didn't want to acknowledge it, a little seed of worry was now rooted in my heart.

Living back in the country was fun. The boys loved playing together in the mud, riding bikes, fishing, and digging for crawdads.

Our home also had a large game room that functioned as Rick's office by day. But the real action kicked in at night when the foosball and pool table came alive. Friends from the community constantly dropped in for a game and a drink.

I didn't mind this at all because I loved a good game of pool! When I was a kid, my dad took a trip to Texas and happened upon a beautiful slate-and-marble pool table for sale. Willie Nelson reportedly played on it. Daddy brought it home where it took pride of place in the center of our living room.

I learned how to execute showy shots behind my back, jump the cue ball, and put left or right English with the best of them. Now I had fun trying to give Rick a challenging game every chance I got. We would laugh and tease each other, and I had the sneaking suspicion he was *probably* letting me win most of the time when I did.

The first couple of months flew by as we juggled the usual "getting to know each other" routines and the challenges of blending a ready-made family. We also spent a lot of time driving. Rick's daily round-trip commute was thirty miles, and mine was sixty miles. In addition, we took the boys to sports practices, games, and birthday parties.

I kept waiting for things to more or less settle into a routine, but obstacles continued to pop up. For one thing, the remodeling work on the house stretched ahead with no end in sight. Art and his crew showed up every day to commence hammering.

Tarps and tools felt like a permanent part of the décor. I would dodge and weave around their ladders with my baskets of laundry, trying to pretend I didn't mind having people constantly roaming throughout the house.

In addition to the construction buzz, we had Rick's CPA clients coming and going at the home office. Rick seemed to view this as completely normal. I knew it was part and parcel of customer service, but the continual flow of visitors became a low-grade irritant.

I was also astonished to discover how much time and man power the poultry operation consumed. Every seven weeks or so, the poultry producers delivered approximately one hundred twenty thousand baby chickens fresh from the hatchery.

Between the remodeling crew, the poultry operation, and the accounting business, my life became a 24-7 revolving door. Feed trucks rumbled in at all hours of the day and night, headlights beaming down the driveway toward the dining-room window.

I hadn't expected this but tried to understand and make the best of it.

However, my tiny seed of worry now felt like a tense, little root ball extending further every day. We were so busy that Rick and I barely saw each other. Even worse, he didn't seem to care.

I longed for time with my new husband to nurture our fledgling relationship. I quickly learned, though, that everyone else wanted a piece of him too. As soon as I tried to start a conversation, his cell phone would ring, or his beeper would shrill.

"I need to get this," he'd say, disappearing out the door to someplace quieter. I would putter around a while, hoping he'd finish up quickly and come back. But that hardly ever happened. Soon enough, I got used to just heading to bed and falling asleep long before he came in.

At first, I felt confused and tried to rationalize away my hurt. *It's just the usual "settling in" period every marriage goes through, Cindy. It's not that he doesn't want to spend time with you—there's just so much on his plate. Be thankful he's such a hard worker.*

My tendency to find the silver lining and minimize difficulty was a strong habit learned in childhood. I had always been a "stuffer." I wouldn't call myself a doormat, but I dreaded conflict. To avoid any whiff of uncomfortable confrontation, I'd just keep stuffing my hurt down inside—*stuff, stuff, stuff.*

But the pressure kept growing. By now, I lived my life in compartments—juggling between various, fragmented versions of Cindy. At work, I was Cheerful-Competent Cindy. When talking with Momma, I became Optimistic-Upbeat Cindy. For Tyler, Brooks, and Farron, there was always Loving-Mom Cindy. But all Rick needed during our brief interactions was Undemanding-Accommodating Cindy.

I was trying my best to make sense of everything. I desperately longed for our relationship to work somehow. But things only got worse.

Rick started coming home later and later. The first time, I nearly panicked. *Where is he? What if he's been in a car wreck?* I wasn't sure I should call—I didn't want to rock the boat and make him upset by sounding like a nag. But it finally grew late enough that I dialed his cell.

"Yeah," he answered.

"Hey there," I said, trying to sound normal. "I hope everything's OK?"

"Oh, I'm just driving around."

I was stupefied. "Driving? Where?"

"On some back roads. I need a break from all the people there—the clients, the remodel crew—everything. I just need to take it easy for a while. Don't wait up for me."

I hung up the phone in shock. I knew he was avoiding me.

This was too big to stuff down anymore. So I shifted into denial. *It's all the stress at the office and home—it's just getting to him. Don't take this so personally, Cindy—plenty of other people go through this too. He's just coping with being a newly married man and checking in with his good old boys. It will pass eventually.*

But each day brought new hurts, and it grew harder to believe my own excuses. We were only three months into our marriage—this should have been the best time of our lives. I shouldn't be lying alone in the dark, night after night, with another broken dream staring me in the face. *What's wrong with me? Why can't I fix this?*

I still didn't want to cause a scene or a confrontation. I just wanted my husband back. If I kept quiet, maybe that would happen.

One day, Rick announced some news that felt like a reprieve. He was going to merge his accounting businesses and work full time from his office at the farm.

At first, this seemed like a great plan.

Rick will be less stressed, I thought with relief. *And I won't be driving home to an empty house every night. We'll have more time together. Maybe Rick will even come to church with me now.*

Before we married, I attended Family Church, a nondenominational church in Pine Bluff. Once we came back from our honeymoon, I'd planned to start again.

However, Rick showed no interest in going. He claimed he was too busy—and I certainly didn't want to go alone. How would I answer all the questions about why my wonderful, new husband wasn't in church with me?

Now he would be working from home, and I fervently hoped for a fresh start. However, it quickly became apparent that things were deteriorating even faster.

His drinking increased, and he'd long since dropped the pretense of not smoking around me. He called it "just messing around with cigarettes."

New faces began showing up around the house at all hours—men with hard eyes towing aloof girlfriends who ignored me. Rick would head out the door with them and be gone all night.

When I drummed up my courage to timidly ask if everything was OK, he brushed me off. I didn't push.

I felt like we were in a conspiracy of silence, pretending that our marriage wasn't eroding before our eyes. The gaping rift between us developed so rapidly that it could hardly be denied, yet we weren't acknowledging any of it.

Our days gathered ominous momentum like a runaway roller coaster; little moments of reprieve followed by another plunge into despair—always deeper and more cutting than the last.

Rick knew just when to pull in the reins on his behavior. When Brooks and Farron were home, he shined like a superstar. In those times, I'd think, hopefully, *If he would just talk to me, maybe I could help him.*

But I was afraid to push for a real conversation. My default setting was to avoid conflict. Rick often reinforced that by saying to me, "If you don't expect too much out of me, I won't let you down."

It seemed like what he was really saying was, "Don't meddle. Don't ask. Mind your own business, and everything will be fine." I stuffed it all down—and life continued spiraling out of control with no accountability margins in sight.

Sometimes I prayed desperate little prayers. *God, I don't understand what's happening here. What am I doing wrong?* But He never answered in any way that I recognized. I felt like both Rick and God had abandoned me and our marriage.

Finally, I faced my worst suspicions. Rick had to be doing drugs.

I didn't think his abrupt, bizarre changes were alcoholism alone. Rick's intense reversal happened over mere weeks and escalated dramatically.

I suspected meth, and my thoughts tumbled relentlessly.

Where is he getting the drugs? When did he start? I know he's lying about so many things. What should I do? Should I confront him with his deceit?

For the first time, I began to feel real anger. *Does he think that somehow I'm not going to know as long as he doesn't do the drugs in front of me? Does he think he's being smooth about this? Where is he hiding his stash?*

All the stress wound me tighter than a clock. There was no way out.

One afternoon, I walked into the house with little Tyler. We had stopped in to pick up a few things before driving to meet my parents halfway between my house and theirs. Tyler was going to spend the weekend with them.

I discovered two strange women making themselves right at home *cooking in my kitchen*! All my fear and anger started spewing out as I told them to leave. They stared right back at me and said Rick hired them to paint the house, and they'd leave when they were finished.

I was livid.

Rick drove up, and I stormed outside to confront him. He barely looked at me. His only response involved walking into the kitchen and asking the women to leave "for the day."

I was seething. *"For the day"? You've got to be kidding me!*

By the time I reached the meeting place with my parents, I was a hot mess and crying.

My dad immediately took Tyler while Momma and I went into the bathroom. I unloaded—everything came pouring out. Momma was devastated, almost in shock. She didn't want me going back home that night, but I assured her I'd be OK.

I knew I couldn't take much more, but I needed a plan.

We finally said our goodbyes, and they left with Tyler. Momma brought Daddy up to speed later that night, and I can only imagine his response.

Rick disappeared again. It was the longest he'd ever been gone. As usual, he didn't answer my calls. By then, I hardly cared.

Three days later, I arrived home from work and walked in through the breezeway. Two guys I'd never seen before stood in my kitchen. We looked at each other in silence.

"Where's Rick?" I finally asked. One of them pointed down the hall toward the game room.

When I walked in, Rick was leaning against the pool table with a faraway checked-out look in his eyes.

"Where have you been?" I asked quietly.

He stared at the floor. "I went to Memphis to buy some antique records."

I was so sick of his lies.

Before I could say anything, he looked up—directly into my eyes—and said, "I think we should go our separate ways."

My head swirled. A jumble of questions flooded my brain, but no words came out of my mouth.

"Oh, OK," was all I could muster. My mind and body felt numb.

Rick walked past me and down the hall. I heard the door slam as he and the two guys left the house.

I stood in the empty silence, feeling detached. I knew the pain would hit hard later, but for now, I felt only a distant mix of devastation and relief. The decision was made. He had told me to leave, and I knew it was time to make my exit.

The days ahead brought cycles of tears, pain, and endless tormented questions. I felt like I'd just emerged from a surreal whirlwind.

What has happened in less than five months to turn my husband from a loving, caring, responsible man into a cold, withdrawn stranger?

The answer wasn't long in coming.

Chapter 4

Raw reality hit hard the next morning. *What will I tell my friends at work today?* I took a deep breath as I swiped my badge through the time clock and headed toward the locker room. I resolved to say as little as possible. After all, I prided myself on my great ability to cover up trouble. This wasn't my first rodeo by a long shot.

Rick and I are separated, the overwhelming scenario kept flooding my heart with crushing pain as the day dragged on and on.

By the end of the shift, I could no longer ignore the questioning glances from my closest coworkers. *They know,* I thought, and decided to briefly share my sad news.

As soon as I choked out, "We're over," I started sobbing. Within seconds, their comforting arms enveloped me, and reassuring words of support poured over me.

Finally pulling myself together, I thanked them and clocked out. I urgently needed to find someplace for Tyler and me to live.

Rental units were alarmingly scarce, but I'd managed to locate a possibility and make an appointment to see it that afternoon. I hoped to sign the agreement right away before anyone else snagged the unit.

Changing out of my scrubs, I dashed to my little, red Toyota Camry and blazed onto 40th Street, headed for 28th Avenue. My mind drifted as I weaved in and out of traffic. *How did this happen? We were so in love. We had a future planned. Why did Rick change so drastically—so fast?*

The lack of answers ate away at me while my future seemed bleak and empty.

When I arrived at the apartment complex, I cringed. The building looked run-down, and the neighborhood felt ominous.

The apartment manager greeted me with a friendly smile. "Hey sugar, how's your day going?" she asked.

"It's OK, and yours?"

"Oh, I can't complain, wouldn't do any good anyway." *My sentiments exactly.*

"So, whatcha got for me?"

"Well, it ain't much, sugar, but I think you'll like it. Didn't you say you had a little boy? I think it's perfect for you both!" She motioned for me to walk up the stairs first.

I was already uncomfortable with the location, and my uneasiness grew as we passed some seedy-looking tenants. Their coarse words and rough conversation felt like ten-pound weights shackled to my ankles as I trudged up the steps toward my new home.

The kind manager inserted the key and proudly opened the door.

She tried to flip on the light, but the bulb was burned out. "We'll get that taken care of right way, sugar. Go ahead and look around."

Daylight filtered through grimy windows revealing a small space in much disrepair. I fought back the tears as I tried to visualize living in that dark, depressing place. *Maybe I can fix it up and make it nice. Wait,* no, *I can't do this. I can't bring Tyler here!*

I heard the manager speaking, but her words barely registered over my jangling thoughts. "What do you think, sugar? Do you like it? Hey sugar, are you OK?"

"I'm sorry, what did you say?" I tried to focus on her sweet Southern voice.

"Do you like it?" she asked again. "When would you like to move in?"

"I'm sorry, yes, I mean no—I don't think it's what I had in mind. I appreciate your time, but I need to keep looking."

She looked surprised. "Well, call me soon if you don't find what you're looking for, sugar. This won't stay vacant long."

Pray Big

Even though I was relieved to get out of there, I felt afraid as I drove away. *What am I going to do now?*

Suddenly, I remembered some nice duplex units on the other side of town in White Hall, where my friend lived. Could something possibly be available there? Maybe a unit that hadn't been listed yet? Even though it was a long shot, I felt impressed to drive over.

Fifteen minutes later, I was in familiar and much safer territory. The neighborhood was peaceful and less congested. I smiled as I saw people walking their dogs and kids playing in the yards. *I think Tyler will really like it here.*

I passed my friend's house and coasted into a quiet cul-de-sac to look around. Right away, I noticed a man shampooing carpet through the open front door of a duplex.

I pulled in behind his truck and walked up to the open doorway.

"Knock, knock . . . hello," I called in a friendly voice, hoping I wouldn't startle him. The loud-humming cleaner powered down, and he swung around. He didn't look pleased to be interrupted. "Can I help you?"

"I sure hope so!" I smiled, "I urgently need a place to rent as soon as possible. It looks like you have a vacancy here."

His expression closed up even more, and he shrugged his shoulders. "I'm sorry, but I can't help you. I have a waiting list a mile long. You're not going to find *any* vacancies in this area. Too many people want to live here."

"Please, sir, I'm in a tough situation. My husband asked me to move out yesterday, and it turned my world upside down. My little boy is two years old, and I need a safe place to go. I can pay you a deposit plus the first month's rent right now. Please. I have a good job, and I'll be a very good renter."

As I spoke, compassion crossed his face, and his eyes softened with a slight smile. "Sure," he answered as I finished, "why not. The people living here moved out unexpectedly, and I haven't called anyone on the waiting list yet. You can start moving in tomorrow."

"Oh, sir, thank you so much! I can't tell you how much I appreciate your kindness and understanding." I exhaled a huge sigh of relief as I wrote out the check for him.

Thank You, God, for watching over Tyler and me and providing us a great, safe place to live!

God Can Do So Much More

The prayer formed automatically and almost startled me. I realized I hadn't included Jesus in my life very much over the past several months.

Since I didn't go to church anymore, whole days and weeks could slide past without God even crossing my mind. I had been so absorbed with my marriage and work that I barely gave Him a thought.

Yet here He was—helping me in a huge way. Even though everything in my life felt offtrack and lost, was God somehow out in this wilderness *with* me—looking after me?

I could almost hear Papaw's voice drifting across the years, *"Now let us have a little talk with Jesus, let us tell Him all about our troubles."*[1]

I could hardly imagine that kind of close conversation. I had felt *so* alone for *so* long. Could this safe, beautiful apartment *truly* be His way of showing me I hadn't slipped out of His care?

As I drove away, I felt the hot sting of tears building. One after another, they raced down my cheeks and dripped onto my shirt. I gave in and let the sobs come.

I had always loved the picture that came to mind with the phrase "a little talk with Jesus"—a secure friendship with God.[2] But it felt too much like wishful thinking—certainly too risky to believe.

Maybe *some* people knew how to talk with God in ways that brought peace and comfort, but I certainly didn't know how—and I was too scared to try. What if I trusted something and then found out it didn't even exist? I had just been down that road with my marriage. I didn't need any more painful disillusionment.

It was easier to pull myself together and slog ahead on my own. *This is only another bump in the road, Cindy. You'll be OK*, I assured myself.

And the picture faded back into the distance.

After we settled into our cozy, new home, life smoothed out to our "new normal." The leaves turned vivid colors while the wind blew sharper and colder.

Tyler happily rejoined his buddies at the hospital daycare, where he'd gone before, and I stayed busy with work and visits home to see my parents. My goal was to avoid periods of free time where I might be tempted to reflect on past mistakes—not because I didn't want to learn and grow but because I had no answers.

I desperately needed to connect with Rick to gain understanding. *Why did he destroy my life so casually? Why did he cut the foundation out from under me with no explanation?* Until I found resolution, I felt locked in a dark haze of confusion and anger, unable to move forward.

I tried calling him at strategic times when he would be available to talk, but, usually, he didn't bother to answer. On those rare occasions when he picked up the phone, he'd make small talk for a couple of minutes and then toss out a quick, "Hope you're OK—gotta run."

This only frustrated me more. I didn't want casual conversation; I wanted answers.

What I *really* wanted was to give him a good piece of my mind. He deserved to hear in stark terms just how badly he messed up my life. Every time I thought about the destruction he created, knots formed in my stomach. I longed for an opportunity to spew my bottled-up frustration all over him.

But other times, late at night, my memories and thoughts would soften. I remembered the man I fell in love with—I adored *that* Rick Mercer with his shining, impressive character and kind voice.

As bad as our situation was, some tiny part of me still hoped he might come to his senses. I felt conflicted when I contrasted our recent pain with the man who'd once been so thoughtful and kind.

I still dreamed of our marriage somehow being restored—that we could spend the rest of our lives growing closer to God and each other.

But, eventually, I'd jolt back to my present harsh reality, and those wishful moments would shrivel up like dry leaves and fall away. As winter settled in, I more often obsessed over all the wrongs perpetrated against me, diligently cultivating my toxic brew of resentment.

One day I decided to drive out to the farm and confront Rick. When I arrived, I was shocked at how run-down he looked.

Although he was surprised to see me, he invited me in. As I stepped through the door, I felt like I'd entered a twilight zone. Quilts hung over all the windows, making it as dark as a cave. There was strange music playing in another room, and the dense odor of stale smoke and empty beer cans smothered me.

This was no longer the home of a wonderful little family. This was an alternate universe inhabited by greedy strangers bleeding Rick's generous nature and draining his money. They were ostensibly hired for the remodel projects, but little work was being done.

Rick was in no condition for any kind of a talk, and I left feeling hollow and sober.

I called a mutual friend, knowing he was in regular contact with Rick and would have more information.

"It doesn't look good, Cindy," he told me sadly. "Rick's running with a really bad crowd."

Days later, another friend confirmed my worst fears.

Rick was using crystal meth and deteriorating rapidly. He started a couple of months after we married and swiftly plunged from snorting to smoking to shooting up.

Rick lost himself in a crippling addiction that gutted his identity as a responsible and respected man and wreaked devastation on everyone he loved.

His CPA business clientele, the home renovation dreams, and the empire he worked so hard to build weren't important to him anymore. All he wanted was the drug.

As a result, Rick lost his marriage, his entire CPA practice, most of his hard-earned money, and nearly all of his reputation. Some of the grifters living with him drained his bank accounts and began bouncing hot checks all over town. Rick's stunning collapse reverberated throughout the community and left everyone reeling.

During the months of Rick's disintegration, Donna remained my hairstylist. We would hug silently and look into each other's eyes. There were no words for the deep sadness we both carried.

My grief held an additional edge because I finally concluded our marriage was truly over, and I filed for divorce. My heart felt bleak and empty like the short, dark days of winter that now stretched slowly into weeks and then months.

With his life in shambles, Rick realized that the horrible influence of his current circles only tempted him to delve deeper into disastrous choices. He knew he needed to escape and felt the safest choice was to move in with his parents.

Sam and Brenda had always been there for him through the years, and everyone hoped this reprieve would start him toward recovery. With his momma keeping a tight rein on him, Rick didn't have easy access to the drugs. Plus, his old crowd weren't apt to visit his parents' house either.

After his move, Donna continued to update me during hair appointments.

With thankfulness, she'd report how Rick was slowly regaining control of his life. Other mutual friends confirmed that his life now seemed calmer.

Deep inside, I felt truly happy for him. Even though I was still hurting, I genuinely wanted the best for him, Brooks, and Farron. While the CPA business was gone and never to be resurrected, the poultry operations continued and fun times with his boys marched on.

Truth be told, the encouraging reports about Rick's turnaround brought my conflicted thoughts back to life. Although I'd filed for divorce, I wasn't even sure what I wanted anymore.

Sometimes, I'd remember my grand life dream. In those moments, I wondered if I was quitting too soon. Was there a chance for our marriage now that Rick had stopped using meth?

I remembered the joyful scenes when we first met, especially the way our hearts connected so effortlessly. I *still* longed for that deep down—it's *so* hard to abandon dreams.

Other times, however, I just wanted to put this painful episode with Rick Mercer in the rearview mirror and never look back. Our divorce was taking longer than expected, which greatly frustrated me. The closure I was desperately hoping for was taking forever.

The longer it dragged on, the more conflicted I felt. My questions went around and around.

Sometimes I felt a persistent little thought, like a voice calling me to pray—*really* pray—about everything. But the idea of prayer felt like a burden.

For one thing, I didn't know *how* to pray or *what* to pray about. I would quickly push that disquieting little voice away—I didn't want to think about it.

Even if I *had* wanted to pay attention, I knew nothing about real prayer. Where would I start? What could I reasonably expect? The easiest response was to shove that troublesome notion out of my mind as soon as it appeared.

I distracted myself with the reminder that things were back on course for me so far as being a proper Christian. I had started going back to Family Church, and Brother Bill's messages always encouraged me. The people were nice, and my friends welcomed me back.

God Can Do So Much More

I was *comfortable* living as a pop-in Christian—conveniently playing church.

Prayer, on the other hand, felt mysterious and overwhelming, and I had no strength or energy to figure it out.

But that quiet, little voice persisted in random moments, often late at night, calling me to pray when I couldn't settle my swirling thoughts.

How would it feel to stop trying to figure this mess out on your own, Cindy, and go all in with God?

What if you're missing out on something wonderful—something so powerful and miraculous that your life will never be the same again?

That would be some kind of prayer, all right, I'd think wryly.

Hard to even imagine it—a prayer that changes everything.

Eventually, I'd drift off into a restless sleep. The next morning, I'd wake up to get ready for yet another day at work, listening to the cold winter rain. Spring felt impossible and invisible—far off in the distance.

But one of the greatest blessings of my life lay just around the corner.

---

1. Cleavant Derricks, "Just a Little Talk With Jesus," Stamps-Baxter, 1937.
2. Derricks, "Just a Little Talk With Jesus."

Chapter 5

Tyler and I had just finished our evening meal and cozied up on the couch together when I heard a knock on my door.

Hmm, who could that be? I wasn't in the mood for company.

Walking over to peep out the front window, I was surprised to see Karen, a friend from Family Church. *Well, at least she's nice*, I thought. I remembered how she encouraged me when my marriage with Tyler's dad ended.

"Hey Karen, come in, it's great to see you!"

"Hey, Cindy, how are you? Hi there, Tyler, I love your race-car jammies!" Tyler beamed as she joined us on the couch.

After a few minutes of small talk, I asked, "So, what brings you over?"

"Nothing particular," she answered, "I've just been thinking about you and wanted to check in to see how you were doing."

"Oh." *Deep sigh.* "Overall, I'm not too bad."

I tried to sound convincing, but I felt a stinging little tear swim into my eye and then another. I blinked, knowing they screamed *I am not OK!*

Karen was so gentle and understanding. "I know this must be very hard, Cindy. Are you sure there isn't something I can do to help? I don't believe it's an accident that I came tonight. I know God put you in my heart."

"I believe that. Starting over feels so, you know, hard. I know God loves me—I don't doubt that. But I was sure I had found the right one with Rick. Everything fell into place so beautifully. And even though everyone says God always has a plan B and plan C, I just don't want to hear that right now."

"I understand," she answered quietly, and I knew she did. "I'm not here to tell you what to do or even to try and analyze what went wrong. I just wanted to let you know I care and I'm here to help."

Immediately, I felt some of my built-up tension release. I halfway expected some sort of judgmental attitude or lecture from her.

But instead, the Holy Spirit flowed through Karen's words to start me on the path to healing. Suddenly, I felt safe to share with her about the nagging sensation on my heart to pray.

"I'm struggling to utter any words that remotely sound like *real* prayers," I confided. "I feel like my mouth is being held hostage—and I know you find that hard to believe!" I gave a wobbly grin and kept pouring out my heart to her.

"I want to talk to God, and I know I should. But when I attempt to have a serious conversation with Him, I can't find the right words. Has this ever happened to you? My mind wanders all over the place, and I find myself distracted. I can pray for others and pray over my meals without any problem. But I can't seem to connect when it's just me and God one-on-one. Am I making sense to you at all?"

I feared I was rambling. *She probably wishes she'd stayed home*, I thought when I came up for air.

Hurrying to finish, I added, "All of this is just awkward. God probably doesn't have time to listen to any of it anyway."

As I spoke my thoughts out loud, I realized how despairing I truly felt about my *attempted* prayer life. I had read plenty of books about prayer and attended prayer events. But when I needed *real* prayer the most, I felt defeated.

What happened next, however, set the course for one of my greatest blessings ever.

Sensing my deep, crushing burden, Karen placed her hands on my shoulders, looked me square in the eye, and asked a very simple, yet strange, question.

"Cindy, can you say the name *Jesus*?" she asked.

Wait, is this a trick question? I wondered, looking at her oddly.

"Yes, yes, I can," I answered.

"Then just do that—only that," she smiled. "Don't worry about praying any other words. Just say the name of Jesus." Her smile grew wider, "Jesus will take it from there!"

This was quite a surprise. It didn't sound *anything* like how I pictured prayer to be.

I felt skeptical, but she'd been so kind. I certainly didn't have anything to lose.

I nodded my head and said, "OK, I'll give it a try." *Why not, right?*

"Great! I'll see you on Sunday at church. Tell Tyler bye for me," Karen added, as she headed for the door.

After she left, I sat there processing our conversation. I couldn't remember ever crying so much. I knew my tears showed that something powerful was stirring in my heart.

When I thought of her solution, I felt perplexed—but also encouraged. Even though I didn't know how all this would play out, what she'd given me to try wasn't difficult.

It didn't feel hard to say the name of Jesus. I would do it and see what came next.

For the first time ever, I trusted there was possible hope for my prayer life.

The quietness in the duplex seemed unusual after Karen's exit. I turned off the lamp and headed down the hall. Walking into Tyler's room, I found him sound asleep on his blue race-car bed.

Precious boy. I was sure glad he hadn't witnessed my little meltdown. *We're going to get through this, kiddo, somehow. Right, God?* I reached down and kissed my sweet boy on the cheek, tucking him in for the night.

As I climbed into my own bed, I glanced toward the white Bible on my nightstand. My childhood church, Mount Zion Baptist, had given it to me when I graduated from high school.

Through all the moves in my life, I'd kept it close by. Even though I might not read it often, I didn't leave it boxed away. It was very special to me

Now I picked it up and saw my name written all those years ago—*Cynthia June Duncan.* I opened to a random chapter in the New Testament, trailing my finger over several verses.

Then I paused.

I knew I was procrastinating a little because I felt hesitant.

Taking a small breath, almost whispering but still audibly, I said, "Jesus."

OK, that wasn't hard. But seriously, what now?

Suddenly, a melody popped into my head—one I hadn't sung since I was a little girl. I opened my mouth again and let the words flow out.

"Jesus, Jesus, Jesus,

Sweetest name I know,
Fills my every longing,
Keeps me singing as I go."[1]

Something was happening inside me.

Wow, that was different. I'll take more, please!

Since I didn't remember the rest of the song, I repeated those same seventeen words over and over again. Then I read a few Bible verses.

My tentative little sense of something different and wonderful grew a bit stronger.

I remembered how often, back through the years, that I'd find myself thinking, *There has to be something more.* Now I realized I'd just discovered a piece of the answer that I'd been seeking for a very long time.

Jesus *could* fill my every longing. And tonight, right here, He was showing me something very new and precious about prayer.

I didn't need to struggle for the "right" words. I didn't need to make a spiritual presentation.

Just saying the name "Jesus" brought peace and comfort to me.

In the days ahead, I realized nothing about Karen's suggestion was complicated. But I also understood that I *still* faced a challenge—ongoing internal warfare.

Would I follow through?

I knew now He'd heard my longing for *something more.* He'd sent Karen with help—an answer so simple that *anyone* could do it.

"For 'whoever calls on the name of the LORD shall be saved' " (Romans 10:13).

But sometimes simple things are easy to postpone.

Will I still show up, even on busy days? What about on the days when I feel doubt— will I brush aside those empty feelings and trust Him enough to say His name?

More than anything, I wanted to experience the goodness and power of Jesus that I read about throughout Scripture.

He counts the number of the stars;
He calls them all by name.
Great is our Lord, and mighty in power;
His understanding is infinite" (Psalm 147:4, 5).

Pray Big

Providentially, Karen continued to be a part of my life for quite some time. She heard and answered God's call to become my much-needed spiritual mentor and accountability partner.

Sometimes I'd be particularly amazed when she would call or come by *exactly* when I most needed encouragement. Her timing was impeccable. God must have given her a special "Cindy radar" gift. Her friendship and support were invaluable just when I needed them most!

She invited me to join a homegroup that met every other week. Also, my connection with Family Church deepened. Now I was being nurtured by a combination of loving spiritual friends, Bible study, and church.

This was just the shot in the arm God knew I needed—I found new life springing up in me.

Several weeks after Karen's first visit, a strange thing happened.

While finishing up some random unpacking, I came across a box of books that I'd purchased a year before meeting Rick. Oddly enough, one, in particular, caught my eye—*Building Your Mate's Self-Esteem*, by Dennis Rainey.

I turned it over and read, "Self-esteem is either the crippler or the completer of the marriage relationship." The description referenced ten essential building blocks to strengthen your mate and your marriage.

I felt impressed that God wanted me to read it, which baffled me.

So I'm supposed to read a book on learning "practical and effective ways" to love and support the mate I do not have! Oh, and "work together to build a vision for the years ahead"! Come on, God, really?

It certainly wasn't the book I would have picked, but I couldn't deny the strong impression to read it.

Page after page, point after point, the same questions kept running through my mind: *Why am I reading this? Why waste my time?*

Even though the divorce wasn't final, I technically didn't have a mate anymore. The effort seemed futile.

Yet, deep down, I couldn't help but wonder—*What if?*

I kept reading.

God Can Do So Much More

In the meantime, I discovered the journal I began the night I met Rick. Startled, I realized that the one-year anniversary of our first date was fast approaching.

So much had happened in this whirlwind of a year. I had been on the highest mountaintops, only to crash into valleys lower than I'd ever imagined.

At one point, I felt completely alone—hopeless to feel any *real* relationship with either my husband or God.

But now God was answering the cries of my heart. He started me on the first baby steps of a new and deeper walk with Him.

Although my marriage seemed long gone, God was growing closer and more personal in my life.

My little flowered journal held only a handful of entries. But on the one-year anniversary of the night we first met, I picked up my pen and added a few short lines:

March 20, 1998

I prayed Rick would never leave me—God, only You know Your plans for us. Help us to understand and be patient and, most of all, help me.

God continued to grow my prayer experience in amazing ways as spring spread across Arkansas that year. Prayer time during Karen's small-group gatherings became super special—just *hearing* the others pray encouraged me!

Best of all (and much to my surprise), when I prayed *myself*, I experienced something profound. My prayers were bringing a sense of true connection with God.

I began hearing myself string together words and phrases that *only* Jesus could have planted within me—and I realized this change was tied *directly* to how I spent more and more time with my Bible.

I wanted to be a follower of Christ and be transformed into something real and alive. My time in His Word shaped my prayers and led me to deeper heart discoveries day by day.

It reminded me of watching a slow sunrise. Light was dawning on my weary soul.

I couldn't *wait* to see what I would discover next.

---

1. Luther Bridges, "He Keeps Me Singing," public domain.

Chapter 6

My understanding of prayer soon took giant leaps forward. Providentially, God opened my eyes to how *narrow* my thoughts and expectations about prayer were. Basically, I viewed prayer as coming to God for what I needed.

I would present a list of requests to Him—sort of like making a requisition at work or going to a vending machine for a snack. He was a source to supply whatever I felt my situation required.

I'll take that, God, but that other option is not quite so convenient right now, was often my thought.

But the more I studied, the more I saw this as a *transactional* view of prayer. I defined a satisfying prayer experience as a *successful transaction*. I would make a request to God, and He would answer.

When He answered quickly, it felt like a very good transaction.

If the answer took a while, however, the transaction felt stalled. Maybe I wasn't making a good enough presentation. Maybe He'd been answering more important prayers and needed a reminder. I would start revising my words a bit and try placing my order again.

If He didn't answer at all, the transaction fell into the "unsatisfactory" category. Because I wanted to avoid that, I usually kept my transactions small. If He didn't respond, I would shrug it off and move to my backup plan.

Now, I found a new longing growing within me when I came to God in prayer.

I didn't want a *transaction*; I wanted a *conversation*.

I wanted *Him* to communicate with *me*! *How can we actually have a dialogue together?* I wondered.

God sent part of the answer through the excellent teaching of Peggy, Brother Bill's wife, during Bible class at Family Church. We were entering a study in the book of Philippians, and her passion for God always made my heart burn with wonder and awe. "Be anxious for nothing, but in everything by prayer and supplication, with thanksgiving, let your requests be made known to God; and the peace of God, which surpasses all understanding, will guard your hearts and minds through Christ Jesus" (Philippians 4:6, 7).

I realized I was very good at *asking*—a *lot*. I made a *flurry* of little requests known to God every day!

But I failed to incorporate the *praise*—the thanksgiving. I began to fill my prayers with worship—praising Him for who He was, praising Him for listening to me, praising Him for the protection He'd given to Tyler and me that day.

Giving thanks quickly opened my eyes to how *intricately* His presence and blessings wove through my life at every level. The more I thanked and praised Him, the more I *noticed* Him.

I also began to recognize how He communicated with me through His Word. The conversation that I longed for happened when I opened my Bible.

One morning, He brought an especially tender moment of repentance as I read,

> I acknowledged my sin to You,
> And my iniquity I have not hidden.
> I said, "I will confess my transgressions to the LORD,"
> And You forgave the iniquity of my sin (Psalm 32:5).

Right away, I began to confess my sins. I expected to feel the familiar secret shame that always came when I remembered them. But, instead, my heart overflowed as I realized I was safe in His love.

I poured everything into the stream of His forgiveness, feeling His grace flood into all my dark, guilty corners and wash them clean. I had no more need for shame.

I realized that my freedom came when I brought everything to Him through confession. He took it *all*, with no condemnation, and threw it away forever. I stood covered with His righteousness.

Next, God showed me how prayer and time in His Word completely *shifted* His place in my life.

Before, although I loved Him as best I knew how, I viewed Him mostly as an important priority on my calendar, my regular weekly appointments with Him came at church. He fit neatly within those scheduled slots.

But now, He appeared *everywhere* in my days. At any moment, He could pop into my thoughts as I noticed something to thank Him for—or faced a situation where I'd remember a Bible verse just when I needed it most.

And I realized *all* of my choices greatly impacted my ongoing connection with Him—including my friendships and what I put into my mind. I grew more aware of making decisions that *protected* my growing walk with Him. I chose to detach from activities and associations that weren't conducive to character building.

I wasn't perfect by a long shot—I was doing my best, one decision at a time. Week by week, every new step brought wholeness and healing.

Spring flowed toward the edge of summer and our first wedding anniversary approached.

For months, I had zero contact with Rick. Occasionally, I received updates from Donna or a handful of other friends. It seemed he was still on a healthier course, but I remained in limbo so far as any permanent resolution.

Our anniversary came and went. Several times during the day, I picked up the phone to call him, only to ditch the idea. *He wouldn't answer anyway*, I reasoned.

I was surprised to discover this milestone turned out to be less difficult than anticipated. I didn't feel any jagged, wrenching pain—just a confused numbness whenever I remembered how wonderful he'd once been and how it all ended.

But unexpected devastation ripped a new hole in my heart the very next day.

God Can Do So Much More

On May 4, 1998, Momma called to tell me that my beloved Papaw had closed his eyes for the last time. I had just lost one of the strongest spiritual towers in my life.

I went through the motions at work on autopilot, pushing my grief aside until I got home. Then I let the tears come. I thought of how he'd hugged me as we swayed on the porch swing, all safe and cozy.

We wouldn't be having our "little talk with Jesus" together on this earth ever again—and heaven seemed a long way off—how I missed him!

The following day at work, I rushed to the break room in between surgical cases. Suddenly, I came to an abrupt stop.

A beautiful peace lily sat on the floor directly in front of my locker.

Who could that be from? I wondered as I opened the card attached to the deep-crimson bow. My mind went blank with shock.

"So sorry to hear about your grandfather, we are praying for you. Rick and the boys."

A mixture of conflicting feelings began racing through me. On the one hand, I felt touched by the kind gesture.

But on the other hand, I felt unsettled, even angry. I *still* had so many unresolved questions for him. What was I supposed to do with all of my resentment over his months of silence?

I also wondered if the peace lily held any deeper meaning. Why had he reached out like this? I concluded that a small piece of his heart for me remained surprisingly intact.

I mustered the courage to call him and give the obligatory "thanks for thinking of me" routine—on his voice mail, of course. I felt certain that he wouldn't take the call based on past times.

Much to my surprise, he answered.

My first instinct was to hang up. Then I thought, *Here's my chance! Let him have it, Cindy!*

But as badly as I wanted to unload, all the rehearsed lines of chastisement wouldn't come. We just chatted for a few minutes about the boys and my Papaw.

Strange as it was, it felt refreshing to hear his voice. He truly sounded great and seemed to be doing well.

As I listened to how his life was back on track, I was genuinely happy for him. But near the end of our conversation, I got my second jolt of the day.

"I'm sorry, Cindy," he said quietly.

My thoughts scrambled while he continued speaking. "I don't know how life got so crazy for me. One thing led to another and, before I knew it, I was sinking so fast. There was no point of return."

How do I respond? I wondered. *Am I supposed to say, "Oh, that's OK, I understand"? Or should I go with, "Do you realize how badly you hurt me?"*

Nothing seemed appropriate in that fragile moment.

I thanked him for the apology and told him I appreciated him thinking of me during the difficult days that lay ahead with the funeral.

After we hung up, I realized the conversation felt healing. I had waited so long for this apology, and I appreciated the way he shared his own confusion and disappointment so openly.

The peace lily marked a turning point. Slowly, Rick and I began talking on the phone again; just here and there at first—but then more and more.

Our conversations went deep as we sorted through some of the details of what went wrong. Perhaps my medical training made me more compassionate—more able to understand how a drug addiction ravages someone, destroying their very personhood.

Now I saw again the Rick Mercer I'd first met and fallen in love with; I suspected those feelings were *still* in each of our hearts—albeit under several layers.

Eventually, we decided to take the next step and start seeing each other again. We wanted to test the waters cautiously, so we picked a date to have dinner at my place with the three boys.

In the meantime, Tyler and I took a quick trip to visit my parents. I thought about telling them about Rick and our reconnection efforts, but deep down, I knew they'd understandably be furious. I reasoned it was best to see how the dinner date turned out before I made any upsetting announcements.

The long-awaited evening finally arrived. I am pretty sure my heart was beating harder than the night of our blind date.

Of course, both Tyler and I were excited about seeing Brooks and Farron. I tried to decide if I felt the same way about Rick.

I don't think I can truly say I'm excited, I considered. *Maybe curious, anxious, and nervous. But am I excited? No. And Mom and Dad would die if they knew!*

Ready or not, the knock on the door jolted me out of my thoughts and back into reality.

"Hey, guys! It's great to see you," I greeted them. *"Great to see you"? Really? I'm scared to death!* "Come on in; I sure hope you're hungry. I have a big pan of lasagna for you, boys!"

Cooking wasn't a natural affinity of mine, but I could make a pretty mean pan of lasagna. Pairing it with salad and garlic bread ensured a great meal for all five of us.

Rick and I awkwardly exchanged hugs and fumbled through small talk for a few moments. Tyler, Brooks, and Farron chattered away as if nothing had ever happened.

But I keenly felt the difference. A *lot* had changed during the last ten months of separation. Thankfully, I had some last-minute dinner preparations to finish, so I left Rick and the boys to visit.

The meal together was a success and went easier than anticipated. The boys were starving, and their chitter-chatter helped melt away my uneasy nerves.

If only we could pick up from here and let all the water under the bridge flow away.

After Rick helped me clear the food and dishes, we sat together on the couch. I knew we were about to attempt an important discussion. Thankfully, the boys were wrapped up in their play outside. They were a safe starting point for our conversation.

"The boys have missed each other—it's great to see them so happy," I began with a deep sigh. "So, what about us, Rick?"

"The last few months have been rough, as you already know. Things really got out of control. But now I'm finally getting it all back together. It's really good to see you, Cindy. How are you doing?"

"We're doing OK. Better than expected. It's taken a little while, but we're making it. I started going to church again. Tyler loves going, and it's been really good for us."

Even as I spoke, I thought again about unloading some rapid-fire comments regarding my hurt, confusion, and pain. But the cutting words wouldn't come.

Instead, I listened to Rick as he shared deeper details of his journey. Just hearing his explanations helped unravel some of the mystery I'd struggled with for months. His openness did a lot to diffuse my internal struggle.

Our serious conversation was interrupted by three little boys bursting through the back door needing a drink to cool down. It was getting late, and Rick prepared to leave. Even as they obediently put away Legos, the boys begged to stay longer.

When the time came to say goodbye, Tyler and I stepped outside to see everyone off. Rick and I were both startled by how ominous the sky looked.

A tremendous crack of lightning and a sudden deluge sent us all darting back inside. South Arkansas was no stranger to intense storms. A quick check of the weather showed a long line of thunderstorms heading our way.

Within minutes, our dinner date and "taking it slow" approach turned into an overnight campout. I surely hadn't seen *this* scenario coming.

The boys were *beyond* excited—blissfully unaffected by the storms bearing down upon us. Playtime resumed in high gear.

I decided to make the best of it.

Back to the kitchen, I went to whip up snacks for everyone. Meanwhile, the boys draped blankets and sheets all over Tyler's room, proudly showing off their "camping fort" for the night.

Admittedly, we all had a great evening. I even felt a tiny bit of hope that possibly, maybe, my dreams could be resurrected one day.

But I wasn't holding my breath.

The next morning, a beautiful sunrise greeted us. The storms were well past, and everything dripped clean and fresh in the warm light as we said our goodbyes. This first little step seemed successful, but I didn't know what came next.

As the days and weeks rolled on, I continued to wonder what any future with Rick might hold.

Meanwhile, I passionately pursued my journey with Jesus and added something more to my daily worship. During my prayer time, I read Bible promises and inserted my name into the verses. Early on, I was led to Ephesians 3:20, 21: "Now to Him who is able to do exceedingly abundantly above all that we ask or think, according to the power that works in us, to Him be glory in the church by Christ Jesus to all generations, forever and ever. Amen."

I would write the promises in my prayer journal, substituting my name.

God Can Do So Much More

Now to Him who is able to do exceedingly abundantly above all that Cindy *asks or thinks, according to the power that works in* her, *to Him be glory in the church by Christ Jesus to all generations, forever and ever. Amen.*

Then I prayed the promise out loud—using the very Word of God to shape my own words.

Lord, You are able!
   Lord, You can do exceedingly abundantly great things—You can do what I cannot imagine.
   You long to surprise us with Your goodness and love.
   I am thankful for the Father, Son, and Holy Spirit, who are working on my behalf so that others will see Your glory! Amen.

At first, this felt awkward. But soon, I considered it a great blessing—another wonderful way to communicate in prayer. I knew that God showed me this spiritual exercise to grow my connection with Him.

I also felt God softly working in the deepest wounds of my heart. The more I absorbed God's Word and engaged in prayer, the more the Holy Spirit offered restoration and healing through *His* power.

Rick's explanations and sincere apologies were integral for heart repair, but they couldn't take away my hurt—only Jesus could do that.

I loved the words of Isaiah 53:5, which revealed that our Savior was wounded for our transgressions and bruised for our iniquities; He was despised *to bring us peace*, and *by His stripes, we are healed.*

Only Jesus could perform the healing in my heart that would allow Rick access once more.

While in this "waiting room" of life, I trusted God with a very bold prayer one night after reading a powerful passage during my devotional time.

Turn Yourself to me, and have mercy on me,
For I am desolate and afflicted.
The troubles of my heart have enlarged;
Bring me out of my distresses!
Look on my affliction and my pain,
And forgive all my sins (Psalm 25:16–18).

Pray Big

Instead of saying my bedtime prayer, as usual, I wrote my prayer in ink right beside the verse in the devotional book, along with the date and time:

July 14, 1998, 11:20 P.M.

Lord—You know the desires of my heart. I ask boldly today for Rick's deliverance and salvation and the restoration of our family.
In Jesus' Name,
Amen.

I soon discovered the next turn on my life path required *every bit* of my new faith just to keep my feet under me.

Chapter 7

A few weeks after our dinner, I experienced one of the most shocking days of my life.

It began like every other day—with my morning devotional time with Jesus. Joy welled up within me as I read God's Word and interspersed prayer moments with Scripture. "So then faith comes by hearing, and hearing by the word of God" (Romans 10:17).

More and more, I learned to trust God with every detail of my life. It dawned on me that God's promises did not end with question marks. Instead, they ended with periods—or even exclamation points! This brought great encouragement because it made His promises really *feel* like promises—like I could count on them. "For all the promises of God in Him are Yes, and in Him Amen, to the glory of God through us" (2 Corinthians 1:20).

My relationship with God was now on a consistent track, and I felt a great sense of hope.

Was I perfect, or did I have it all figured out? No way—not by a long shot. But it was refreshing to see my life moving forward in a good direction.

By contrast, my future with Rick remained a mystery despite our recent reconnection. *What was all that about anyway? Lord, I need You to hold my hand and help me understand.*

Pray Big

I headed into work at the surgery center, knowing a busy schedule was in store. My assignment for the day was working in the cystoscopy room. We had multiple procedures assigned, and moving fast was essential to keep the ball rolling. On days like this, lunchtime came late, if at all.

At around two o'clock in the afternoon, I ran to the break room and stuffed half a bagel in my mouth before rushing down to the operating room suite to prepare for the last patient. Thankfully, the end of the day was almost in sight.

I bent down to adjust the doctor's foot pedal for the procedure table and suddenly felt my head spinning out of control as I stood up again. An odd feeling came over my entire body.

Whoa! What was that? I don't have time to be sick. I'm just hungry, I reasoned. Pushing it aside, I hurried out to get my last patient.

After the procedure, I went to the break room to eat my lunch. Whatever had caused my sudden onset of dizziness seemed to have passed. But a niggling little concern kept circling through my mind.

It's not flu season. But could I be pregnant? Absolutely not! But, what if, wait—there's no way that one night during the storm could possibly . . . ! I could barely form the thought.

I never intended on Rick staying overnight during the storm—things just evolved. *And*, we were *still* married—somehow.

Dear Lord, I don't have time for this! I don't even know for sure if our marriage is salvageable. Please don't let me be pregnant. This would not be good. Amen.

With a myriad of thoughts swirling, I quickly finished my remaining duties for the day. Tyler's grandparents picked him up from daycare, freeing me up for the evening.

So, I did what any responsible young woman would do with sudden onset dizziness *and* the *slight* possibility of pregnancy. I made a very casual date with not one but two pregnancy test kits. Even though I was a bit concerned, my attitude remained cavalier because I felt certain this was most likely a little virus.

With some delicious takeout vegetable fried rice and my pharmacy sack in hand, I had the makings for a great evening. My goal was to dispel the notion of pregnancy right away so I could focus on more important things. I determinedly ignored the small twinge of fear trying to fight its way to the top.

Arriving home, I made a beeline for the bathroom. I quickly took the first test and settled in for the long two minutes of wait time. Within seconds, two positive lines were revealed. Alarm washed over me. *You* have *got to be kidding! This must be a faulty test!*

Because false positives are possible, I waited the full two minutes hoping one line would disappear. It didn't. Then I took the second test. Again, two positive lines appeared within seconds.

Great, just great, Cindy.

A nasty storm brewed outside with heavy wind, thunder, and lightning. Inside, my apprehension grew while my thoughts spiraled wildly.

What will I do? What will Rick think? Will he even care? I waited two more *long* minutes to be sure. Maybe one of the lines would go away.

But nothing changed—*nothing*, except for my whole life. *I don't know what You are thinking, God, but please help me get through this. I don't know what to do.*

I immediately picked up the landline phone to call the only person in the world who would understand—my mom. Unfortunately, the phone service had been knocked out by the storm. I placed my head in my hands and sobbed for what seemed like an hour.

Finally, I managed to pull myself together and drove over to my girlfriend's house. The horrible storm was still going strong, but Kristi only lived a few miles away. We had been through quite a bit together, and I trusted her completely.

I was so upset that I ran up the stairs to her back door and barged into her house without even knocking! She was standing in her kitchen and was quite startled to see me.

"Kristi, you aren't going to believe what's happened to me. I'm pregnant!" I will never forget the look on her face as soon as the words left my lips.

"Cindy, don't joke around like that." After I didn't respond, she said, "Really?"

"I wish I were making this up, Kristi, but two positive pregnancy tests later, here I am. Remember the night Rick and the boys came over? Well, I didn't tell you they ended up spending the night and, well—you know."

"Oh girl, this is crazy! What are you going to do? Have you told Rick?" she asked.

"I don't know what I'm going to do! I'm in total shock, and my phone lines are down at the house. I was going to call my mom, but it's probably best I didn't. She has no idea that Rick and I were even talking, much less had a date. Are your phones working? I need to call Rick right now."

"Yeah, sure, go ahead," Kristi's tone was skeptical even as concern filled her eyes. Clearly, she didn't hold out much hope for his reaction.

"Kristi, I know what you're thinking—and rightfully so. But you know I loved him, and I never wanted our marriage to end. Lately, some changes have happened in his life, and I'm encouraged about his intentions to get his life back on track. We've been making some strides to start over. Now that I'm pregnant, there's another life to consider. In one way or another, we're going to be a family. Tyler, Brooks, and Farron will have another sibling. I feel like I should at least stay open-minded that it could work."

I nervously dialed my mother-in-law's number—Rick should be there. I needed to get this over with and then figure out the next step. She answered, "Hello."

"Hey Brenda, this is Cindy. Is Rick available to talk?"

"No, hon, I'm sorry. He isn't here right now."

"OK, well, I have something very important to tell him. Brenda, I'm pregnant, and I need him to call me right away. Can you give him the message as soon as you see him, please?"

There was a moment of silence before she responded. I could hear the doubt in her voice and knew she also didn't hold out much hope about his response. I thanked her and hung up.

Kristi jumped in as soon as I put the phone down. "Well, that went about as good as you expected, huh?"

"I suppose. Oh Kristi, what am I going to do? He probably won't call back, and even if he does, what then? I have to call my mom. I know she will insist I move back home. Honestly, that seems like a logical solution. But I can't think straight right now."

I started sobbing again, courtesy of my pregnancy-enhanced emotions.

Suddenly Kristi's phone rang. We looked at each other, and my heart began to race. Kristi picked up the phone. "Hello, Rick . . . Yes, she's right here."

Filled with apprehension, I put the phone to my ear.

"Cindy, are you really pregnant?" Rick asked right away.

"Yes, it's true. I took two pregnancy tests, and they were both positive," I replied.

"Cindy, listen. I know I've let you down. I've been a horrible husband, and I'm sorry." Rick seemed to draw a long breath and pause. Then he spoke words I will always remember. "Cindy, I have needed something to wake me up and get my attention. I can't believe you're pregnant, but it's OK . . . I promise you I will spend the rest of my life being the best husband you've ever had. I don't have all the answers, but God will help us."

I began to cry. I couldn't speak. I wanted so much to believe everything he was telling me—to know in my heart that it was the truth.

I don't remember the rest of our brief conversation, but Rick concluded, "I'll be there tomorrow after you get off work to move you back home."

We said goodbye, and I hung up the phone. I knew a lot was about to change—again.

"Well, what did he say?" Kristi was anxious to know the details.

"Kristi, I know this all seems outrageous, but Rick says that this is just what he needed to get his attention. He said a lot of things to me, and I really want to believe him. He said he would be the best husband ever—and, I believe he meant it."

Kristi just looked at me and shook her head. "Oh, Cindy, you aren't going to fall for that, are you? I know you and Rick had something great at one time, but now, I don't know. I'm really worried about you, Cindy. We need to pray."

I thanked Kristi for her love, support, and prayers and went back home. Thankfully, the storms had passed.

I understood Kristi's concerns, but I wanted to believe with all my heart that Rick meant what he said. I was, and am, no different from most people I know. I wanted *and* needed hope. I wanted to try again to make it work. A lot was at stake—including our three precious little boys and the family they could have. I wanted to protect them.

I also knew there would be lots of questions from people who might not understand, but I was ready. And it seemed like Rick was eager for a new start as well. He said all the right words I desperately needed to hear, *and* he was making plans to take the right actions.

Besides, I'd never been one to give up easily. I didn't just walk away without giving it my all. I hadn't intended on things going this fast, but my persistent, resilient nature wanted to believe that we might become a family again.

I fell asleep that night talking to God about my concerns, hopes, and the possibilities that the next days, weeks, and months would surely bring.

True to his word, Rick arrived at my duplex the next evening. I held my breath a little, wondering if he would follow through. When I saw him, it felt like a great first step toward solid reconciliation. It greatly reassured me and confirmed my decision.

It was hard to believe that almost a year had gone by since we had separated. Now here we were, eager to build a family again despite all the challenges.

It took me several days, but I finally mustered up the courage to make the difficult phone call to my parents. It didn't go well. They were shocked and had nothing particularly positive to say. I understood but trusted with time we would make progress.

Over the next several months, our time together as a family felt encouraging. The boys resumed their fun playing on the farm, and great excitement was in the air as we anxiously awaited the arrival of our new baby.

Life became super busy again, and I dropped into bed each evening exhausted. By default, my Bible study and prayer time gradually became more hit-and-miss.

I wasn't attending church as regularly as before. Rick always encouraged me to go even though he rarely joined me. However, he began to question my sixty-mile round-trip commute to Family Church. He suggested that I try the Methodist church where his mom went and where he attended while growing up. Before long, I was driving five miles down the road to my new church.

The church members, many of whom I remembered from our wedding, were very kind and hospitable and welcoming.

Every now and then, Rick showed up just in time for Brother Rusty's message. Then he'd slip out the back door as the last verse of the hymn was sung.

At least he's here, I thought on those occasions.

Our damaged relationship still needed much repair. We had a lot to learn about each other—and about blending a family. In addition, I couldn't deny my gnawing concerns. I knew Rick drank alcohol and smoked sometimes, but thankfully, he was respectful and smoked outside when I was home.

Despite all of the challenges, we picked up the pieces together. And Accommodating-Optimistic Cindy was committed to making things work, no matter what.

With my due date fast approaching, there were baby showers at work and church. Anticipation built ever higher.

But the large cloud of the strained relationship between my parents and Rick seemed even bigger when contrasted with all of the excitement in the air. I felt more and more frustration—wondering if the rift would ever heal.

I don't remember how it happened, but I'm sure my mother deserves the credit. She always had a way of smoothing things out, and I'm sure she convinced my dad to put the past behind us when the big moment arrived.

On March 23, 1999, we happily celebrated the arrival of Reece Austin Mercer—*all* of my family together. My parents, Rick's parents, Farron, Brooks, Tyler, and a host of friends and other family members welcomed our new addition to the Mercer family.

About an hour after giving birth to Reece, the delivery room was packed with people. I was gushing with joy! Everyone wanted a peek at our precious baby boy!

My heart overflowed as I watched all the built-up tension between my parents and Rick dissolve as soon as Reece entered our world. Everything in our life seemed so perfect. I didn't want it to end.

That evening as I gazed at the miracle God had given us, I recalled the events of the day. Rick was by my side throughout, and my love cup was full. When my husband was sober, he was an amazing man.

If only time could be frozen. I wanted to seize this moment—so peaceful and full of promise—and hold on to it forever.

Surely we'd turned the hardest corner. Surely this new and joyful beginning would become a strong foundation for my updated grand life story. Surely there would be no more major surprises.

Chapter 8

The year following Reece's birth became a kaleidoscope of wonderful memories. We were a brand-new family—with brand-new possibilities. We *loved* our new life together.

Sure, our boys got in typical sibling scuffles, but they lived each day to the fullest, whether they were riding bikes, fishing, or playing in the mud. Rick and I enjoyed watching them achieve milestones in their lives, and we did a lot of fun activities together.

The boys and I faithfully attended Kids Church every Wednesday night, plus Sunday School and church each weekend. I connected with several ladies who were passionate about Jesus, and we formed a thriving friendship, much to my liking.

Before I knew it, I was teaching Bible class and serving in other areas where needed. By spring 2000, I became a member of Union Methodist Church. I loved how they were so kid friendly and welcoming—everyone was on a first-name basis.

As delightful as all of this was, an important chapter of my grand life story continued to elude me—the one where our *whole* family sat together in church.

Rick completely supported my attending and very much appreciated that our boys were growing up with a regular church experience. However, he stayed home more often than he joined us. Usually, he just smiled and kissed us goodbye as he generously slipped me a one-hundred-dollar bill to put in the offering plate.

God Can Do So Much More

Meanwhile, at home, it seemed that Rick and I could never quite settle into fully smooth sailing. Sometimes I'd try to tell myself that all marriages hit bumps in the road. But other times, I'd feel extra sensitive to the fear that maybe we were slowly spiraling in the wrong direction.

And even with the busy connection at my new church, my relationship with Jesus felt like it was slowly shifting into neutral. I was going through the motions. They were good motions but not nearly as fulfilling as I'd hoped.

It felt like a pivotal piece of the puzzle was missing. Although I couldn't put my finger on it, there was a definite yearning to fill the constant, gnawing empty spot in my life. I just wasn't *completely* satisfied. I wanted something more.

In the meantime, I maintained a good church-going-girl persona. I had the routine down perfectly. But my daily devotional times collapsed under the weight of my chaotic schedule. Time didn't afford me the depth of spiritual commitment I once had.

Sometimes I reasoned the strange transition was logical—almost normal. *Surely, God understands the new responsibilities I've taken on*, I'd think.

Being a mom to four active boys was a full-time task, not counting my job at the surgery center. *Maybe later will be a more convenient time to pursue my Jesus journey. Besides, is He even listening anymore?* It seemed fair to assume I'd worn Jesus out with my on-again-off-again approach. Frankly, it drained *me*.

I still loved Him and desired His presence and peace, but life's hectic pace had taken over.

Unable to shake the strange angst in my heart, I immersed myself in something I'd abandoned for a while—reading. I *wanted* and *needed* to know things, so I read as much as possible.

Even as a child, I asked lots of questions. *Why* did God orchestrate certain events? *What* would my future be like? *How* could I know His will for my life?

Many of these questions spilled over into adulthood completely unanswered. Now they impacted issues with Rick. In fact, my marriage was one big ball of recurring questions.

Determined-Seeker Cindy set out to obtain answers once and for all. Praise God, as I returned to reading, I felt His hand guiding me to words of peace. Providentially, a beautiful promise surfaced right on time. "On the last day, that great day of the feast, Jesus stood and cried out, saying, 'If anyone thirsts, let him come to Me and drink. He who believes in Me, as the Scripture has said, out of his heart will flow rivers of living water' " (John 7:37, 38).

Was I thirsty? Oh, yes—I was downright parched! This promise assured me of living water, which I desperately longed for each day. The crucial condition was a *belief* in the One who could *provide* this eternal wellspring of life.

What do You mean, Jesus? I wondered. *Of course, I believe in You!*

The thought immediately came to my heart, *"Do you* really *believe Me, Cindy? Do you believe My power* still *changes things? Do you believe My promises directly apply to* you?"

" *'Lord, I believe; help my unbelief!'* " (Mark 9:24).

Sure, I believed God *could* heal and provide miraculous marriage restorations for *others*. But to believe He could, or even *would*, do that for *me* was quite another story.

Over and over, it seemed as soon as I dared believe my husband might be changing to the man he promised, I was proved wrong and disappointed once more. The climate in our home was unpredictable—just like the Arkansas weather.

And I knew a huge storm was brewing again. Rick's undesirable extracurricular activities showed signs of resurfacing. Clearly, his drinking had increased.

Most days, he was careful to control his booze when the boys were around. Even though my husband was complicated, no one could deny he loved his boys—and they loved him.

I counted those as "good days" and held on tightly to their memory when things went south. We never quite reached a consistent positive streak, and our growing difficulties diluted the sense of security I longed to feel.

My own response to Rick's shenanigans added fuel to the fire because I exploded in a radically different direction. Gone were my days of suffering in silence. Now I almost welcomed every opportunity to caustically unload an arrogant and (to my mind) well-deserved tirade.

With spiteful, harsh tones, I'd tell Rick that he was nothing but an alcoholic. I followed this with a stinging outline of inevitable consequences to his family and business if he didn't get control of his problems. My main goal was to verbally wound and draw blood.

Of course, my words went in one ear and out the other with Rick. Despite that, I continued to sling shrewish accusations as my frustration skyrocketed.

Rick drank fifteen beers every day, and, on select days, he added vodka, tequila, rum, or whiskey. Deep down, I knew his drug use had also returned, even though I never caught him red-handed.

I had become quite the bitter nag and cashed in on every available moment to rake him over the coals about his lifestyle.

My original meek, kind voice was long gone, transitioning over the years to screaming and yelling at him from the top of my lungs. Sometimes I couldn't believe what I heard coming out of my own mouth. I knew that if my church friends could see this side of me, they'd be horrified.

My secret guilt only deepened my inner conflict. I equally hated my carefully adorned church-girl mask and the ugly nag I became in private. I blamed my husband for forcing me into this mess because of his issues.

My former passive attitude had been a great convenience to him, and it now irritated him highly that I was demanding honest answers. I was through covering for him when family and acquaintances would ask the same questions over and over again. My ears were tired of hearing, "Where is Rick? How is Rick? Is everything OK?" Plus, I was about out of excuses.

Fed up with maintaining the facade, I frequently snapped at those who asked the questions—which left me, yet again, disgusted with myself.

One day, a respected gentleman kindly approached me at church. "Cindy, is Rick all right? What's going on with him?" To which I replied, "Please quit asking me! If you really want to know, why don't you ask him yourself?" He was a super-nice guy, and I felt awful for my short temper and curt reply—which, truth be told, was a cry for help. *Please visit my husband; maybe you could make a difference and get his attention.*

But, understandably, most people stayed away—except for a few visits from good-hearted friends who were brave enough to stop by and say hello occasionally.

Over time, the enemy of souls made another strategic attack on my heart.

Because I filled almost every spare moment with an array of spiritual friendships and pursuits, my attitude became falsely confident and superior toward Rick. I cherished the grand delusion that my regular church attendance and flurry of "righteous" activities made me a kind of super saint—*especially* compared to my husband.

With all my church-going and reading, you would've thought my attitude and prayer life would have been stellar. From the outside looking in, I had it all together—or so it seemed. But, sadly, that was far from the truth.

My longing to know and serve God was sincere, but my mouth was perfectly poised for spewing sarcasm toward Rick regularly.

In addition, and without even recognizing it, I slid eagerly into a cesspool of gossip—all in the guise of emotional validation and relief.

I willingly shared the nitty-gritty details of Rick's failings with my church companions, coworkers, and family. When their sympathy came, I felt superior and justified in my actions.

It became so gratifying to focus on all of the problems surrounding me that I forgot to turn my face toward the Great Problem-Solver, Jesus.

Because of my spiritual inconsistencies, I ebbed and flowed from emptiness and unhappiness to occasional rare moments of hopefulness. "Feelings" became my navigational system. It was no surprise my end destination was spiritual negligence.

I was fed up with my husband, and he was fed up with me too. We were both miserable. We fought all the time, and neither of us was willing to call a truce.

Even though my spiritual walk vacillated between moments of self-disgust and superiority, I was especially grateful for the prayers and support of my pastor and friends. Unfortunately, I dropped the ball each time I walked out of the church door.

I was fooling myself to think I could make it without a personal relationship with Jesus. I professed Him with my lips but denied His power.

My prayer life waned until it became virtually nonexistent—a fact undetected by most people. But I knew. I was slowly suffering inside, and something had to change—fast. "Even though our outward man is perishing, yet the inward man is being renewed day by day. For our light affliction, which is but for a moment, is working for us a far more exceeding and eternal weight of glory, while we do not look at the things which are seen, but at the things which are not seen. For the things which are seen are temporary, but the things which are not seen are eternal" (2 Corinthians 4:16–18).

I longed for this inward renewal, but the hopelessness of my life made it seem impossible. We were on a fast slide into devastation. How could we ever come back from this?

Chapter 9

Most days felt like a nightmare interrupted by rare glimpses of the Holy Spirit appearing now and then. On those occasions, the dismal fog surrounding my heart was penetrated by a few radiant beams of hope.

Sometimes, great encouragement came when people shared that they were praying for my situation. On other days, an uplifting card would arrive in the mail just when I needed it most.

These "times of refreshing" always encouraged me to return to my constant, fervent prayer for a miracle: *Dear Lord, please help Rick to change!* And there were *even* a few promising moments with him as well.

One day, I stood at the sink washing dishes when Rick walked in and headed toward the refrigerator. I saw him pause as he opened the door, glancing at a yellow sticky note I'd put there to encourage myself. I could see him reading it. "Faith comes by hearing, and hearing by the word of God" (Romans 10:17).

Suddenly, he asked, "What does that mean to you, Cindy?"

I continued rinsing a dish for a moment while questions flew through my mind. *He wants to know about the scripture I posted. What should I say? Is he mad about it? Is it remotely possible that he's interested in something spiritual?*

"What do you mean?" I responded, stalling for time.

"This note—about faith. I wonder what that means to you and how you think it works."

"Oh, well, it just means that when you read the Bible or listen to sermons where the Word of God is being spoken, your faith in God will increase and become stronger."

He mumbled, "Oh, OK," and walked out the door.

What was that all about anyway? I wondered. *He never asks me about Bible verses. I mean, he did grow up in the church—surely, he knows what that scripture means. Or maybe he already knew and just wanted to have a conversation. Who knows with him.*

A small, hopeful grin formed on my face in response to our odd interaction, and my heart felt momentarily lighter as I gazed out the window watching our boys play whiffle ball in the yard.

A couple of months later, one Wednesday evening after Kids Church, the boys were very tired and went to bed extra early. I settled into bed, hoping to read a little bit before falling asleep. I realized I hadn't spent much time reading Scripture lately.

Reaching over, I picked up my Bible and opened it to the book of Psalms. Within seconds, my eyes rested on a comforting passage. Feeling impressed to jot it down somewhere, I quickly grabbed my journal. My jaw dropped open in disbelief when I noticed almost a year had passed without a single entry. *How can that be? I used to write in here all the time.*

My moment of surprise disappeared as I scribbled out, *"Your word is a lamp to my feet and a light to my path" (Psalm 119:105).*

Then I wrote down the "Cindy translation": *"Simply put, study the Bible so you will be able to stay on the right path and not stumble."* That was certainly clear enough instruction.

Next, I turned to John 5:24 and continued writing, "Most assuredly, I say to you, he who hears My word and believes in Him who sent Me has everlasting life, and shall not come into judgment, but has passed from death into life."

I wanted everlasting life for sure! Paging back to Luke, I wrote in my journal: *The next scripture is awesome and ever so true!*

"But why do you call Me 'Lord, Lord,' and not do the things which I say? Whoever comes to Me, and hears My sayings and does them, I will show you whom he is like: He is like a man building a house, who dug deep and laid the foundation on the rock. And when the flood arose, the stream beat vehemently against that house, and could not shake it, for it was founded on the rock. But he who heard and did nothing is like a man who built a house on the earth without a foundation, against which the stream beat vehemently; and immediately it fell. And the ruin of that house was great" (Luke 6:46–49).

Life was certainly shaky—and, oh, how I longed for solid ground to stand on! I wrapped up my study with Deuteronomy 8:3, "So He humbled you, allowed you to hunger, and fed you with manna which you did not know nor did your fathers know, that He might make you know that man shall not live by bread alone; but man lives by every word that proceeds from the mouth of the LORD."

Sad to admit, but I knew I hadn't been living "by every word"—not even close. I longed to do better. For several minutes I sat lost in thought, reflecting on the significance of what I'd just studied.

Moments later, Rick entered the bedroom and wanted to know what I was reading. Much to my surprise and delight, he was genuinely interested. We had a brief but wonderful conversation about the scriptures I'd written in my journal.

As my husband drifted to sleep, I wrote (with a little smile), *"Rick said he wanted the faith I have." Hmm.*

Deep down, I wasn't sure I had *any* faith left, but apparently, he saw *something* in me that I couldn't see. I was puzzled because Rick shockingly seemed to understand biblical concepts better than me.

Ironically, I wanted *his* biblical understanding, and he wanted *my* faith.

Well, maybe one day with Your help, Lord, Rick and I will have just that. And a happy, normal home life would be wonderful too!

As I closed my eyes that night, I wondered if my prayers would *ever* be heard, much less answered. Yet these small yet significant evidences of His love were a balm to my weary spirit. While I longed and waited for "showers of blessings," I cherished these "mercy drops" that fell now and then.[1]

The very next night, it seemed God was urging me to read Isaiah 55:10, 11.

"For as the rain comes down, and the snow from heaven,
And do not return there,
But water the earth,
And make it bring forth and bud,
That it may give seed to the sower
And bread to the eater,
So shall My word be that goes forth from My mouth;
It shall not return to Me void,
But it shall accomplish what I please,
And it shall prosper in the thing for which I sent it."

If only I'd known the *powerful* truth contained in that scripture—but time and God would have their way in the years to come.

By nature, I'm someone who likes fast results, normally tackling problems with full-steam-ahead energy. Patience usually doesn't feel like a virtue to me—it feels like wasted time.

When I considered these small beams of hope with Rick, I felt a fresh kindling of my enthusiasm to keep seeking for resolution. I would set my mind to uncover the elusive formula that would speedily turn things around once and for all.

My thoughts landed on an idea I'd been entertaining for a while—talking to Brother Rusty. I was certain that if I told our pastor the nitty-gritty details surrounding our marriage, he could surely fix our problems. After all, he "tied the knot" when he pronounced us husband and wife—maybe he could help keep the "knot" from unraveling completely.

Knowing Rick would be furious if I told the pastor our "dirty laundry," I postponed a bit but finely dredged up my courage. Just as expected, Brother Rusty and his wife, Debbie, were very sympathetic. Their prayers brought great comfort, and Brother Rusty kindly began to drop by more often.

Thankfully, Rick was always cordial and commented more than once how much he liked Brother Rusty. This was unusual because my husband was generally skeptical and suspicious of virtually everyone but especially preachers. In his opinion, they were almost all hypocrites.

But as smooth as our visits were with Brother Rusty, nothing much changed with Rick. Clearly, I'd need something more. Moving my "mountain" would take a miracle!

By this point, Rick openly smoked two packs of cigarettes per day. In addition to his smorgasbord of alcohol, I was certain he was using drugs. Unfortunately, my ongoing efforts to catch him "in the act" frustrated me to no end. The closest I came was finding a small bag of marijuana in the pocket of his blue jeans.

Sadly, his erratic and unpredictable behavior indicated he was using far more than weed. Red flags were all over the place, and disaster was on the horizon. For the time being, though, my husband stayed several steps ahead of most people—especially me. He maintained a slick composure and worked hard at keeping control even though he was falling apart inside.

To top it all off, I'd grown painfully aware of a devastating element that especially wounded the deepest part of my spirit—Rick's apparent use of pornography.

In the early years of our marriage, I knew he viewed explicit material on occasion, which I basically ignored. It was just another hurt to stuff down inside.

However, as distance built between us, my pain and sense of rejection grew stronger. His lack of physical interest in me only added to my intolerance, anger, and grief. I plunged deeper into despair, and any remaining trace of intimacy between us was robbed by my suspicions about this detestable intruder poisoning our home.

The inevitability of divorce barreled down on me as we careened toward the abyss. I had no idea what to do next.

My despair finally drove me to take a desperate step.

---

1. Daniel W. Whittle, "Showers of Blessing," public domain.

Chapter 10

For several years, I quietly watched one of the anesthesia providers on staff at the hospital. Actually, you couldn't miss Dave—he was six feet, six inches tall with dark hair and a sunny California smile matching his Birkenstocks. *No one* in Arkansas wore Birkenstocks and shorts in the winter—except Dave.

But what *really* caught my attention was how Dave offered to pray with his patients before their procedures. It was amazing to witness.

He even kept a prayer journal in his scrub shirt pocket. Every day, without fail, I noticed him pull it out and read through the list.

I knew Dave and his colleagues (Doctors Ferdinand, Gary, and Jerry) were Seventh-day Adventist Christians. I had no idea what that entailed, but something was different about them. They didn't laugh at crude jokes, they didn't swear, and they always went the extra mile to be kind and caring.

Although I didn't talk about my personal problems with them, I felt my drastic marriage situation required drastic measures. One day, I finally mustered up my nerve and hesitantly approached Dave.

"Hey, Cindy!" he said, smiling.

"Hey, Dave, . . . I, uh, I was wondering—would you happen to have any room left in your prayer book for a couple more names?"

His smile grew even more kind as he immediately drew it out of his pocket along with a pen.

Outwardly calm, I watched him jot down, "Rick and Cindy Mercer."

Inside, I felt like my heart was slowly breaking apart.

Would enlisting Dave to pray make any difference? My wise friends and spiritual advisers all told me over and over again that Rick would *never* change. And I, of all people, knew why they felt that way.

Now Dave and his prayer book felt like one of my last hopes for a miracle.

Nothing changed, unfortunately. Our marriage lingered on life support, and our thermometer of misery held only two extreme settings—cold and hot. When the boys were around, there was icy silence broken with minimal clipped responses. But when the boys were gone, the scorching heat of my bitter wrath rained down on Rick's drunken head, and full screaming matches erupted often.

There was no holding back the toxic buildup of hatred and heartache spewing out of my mouth every chance I found. Eventually, Rick would slam the door behind him, or I'd run to the spare bedroom and break down in sobs.

Lord, help me out of this nightmare! Please change Rick, I begged over and over into an empty void of silence.

Morning after morning, I dragged myself out of bed, fuzzy-headed, and drove wearily to work. I could see the pity in the eyes of my coworkers. Dave gave me literature a few times, and I thanked him, but I was too overwhelmed to read it.

I knew things were coming to an end for our marriage, and great rolling depths of pain nearly drowned me. Three years together, plus a year of separation, were about to go up in smoke.

By now, even my desperate prayers to change Rick had dried up.

We were barely functioning—casualties of the real-life war fought in our home every day, each of us crippled by the constant verbal attacks. Despair hung in the air.

On top of everything else, I experienced a health scare when my heartbeat started racing uncontrollably for no apparent reason. My doctor diagnosed it as panic attacks and prescribed some steps for relief. Despite implementing his suggestions, the tyrannical ticking of my pulse increased—especially aggravated as I neared home each evening after work.

Finally, my stress reached a saturation point. Physically, mentally, and emotionally, I was empty. There was nothing left to give. The tyrannical cycles between Rick and me left me exhausted. Sadly, discouragement set up like concrete, and I realized that everyone else must be right. Rick would never change.

With a broken prayer and a broken heart, I made the wrenching decision to leave Rick. There was no more hope.

I lay in bed, tossing and turning, knowing that the next day I would again be searching for a place to live. But this time, there would be no looking back—no regrets. Walking away was long overdue.

The dark hours dragged on, and I barely dozed. The thought of returning to single life was a frightening reality, hitting me like a ton of bricks.

A lonely, empty future stretched endlessly ahead, shrouded in a heavy gray fog of pain. In some distant corner of my heart, I wondered if I'd ever feel joy or hope again. "The waters surrounded me, even to my soul; the deep closed around me" (Jonah 2:5).

Chapter 11

ugust 5, 2002

A   My blaring alarm clock shrilled the next day at 5:30 A.M. I slipped out of bed and groggily made my way to the bathroom.

The girl looking back at me in the mirror was worn and tired. Hopelessness faced me each day.

Staring long and hard into the mirror that Monday morning, I chased down my decision to leave. No one could say I hadn't tried. Granted, I wasn't perfect—but I'd given it my all. This moment, facing the death of my dreams, felt surreal.

After washing my face and brushing my hair, I began my normal talk with God. I called it my "prayer time." But it was mostly me talking and telling Him how I wanted things to go—with a few random spiritual thoughts added in. I reasoned this was how everyone talked with God.

I was certainly skilled at these one-way conversations with Jesus, and I expected this one would be no different. I launched in, feeling weak and feeble, angry, and disillusioned—telling Him yet again how miserable I was and how He needed to hurry up and fix my wretched life.

Now that I was about to take the gigantic step of forever leaving my broken marriage, I figured I should hash it out with God in one final prayer—just to be sure my anticipated actions were all in order.

I wanted God's sign-off—His acknowledgment that I'd given Him every chance to change Rick, and clearly, Rick wasn't interested. Now I needed

God to extricate me and lead me to my new life.

I stood alone in the empty quietness and cried out with every ounce of courage I could muster, "Lord, I need a miracle, and I need it now!"

Deep down, I expected the miracle would begin with a divorce. In my mind, the dissolution of our marriage would be the answer to finally provide escape and relief from the pain. After all, my friends and family continually assured me that "everything will get better when you leave."

Now I waited for a sense of divine confirmation—an assurance of the rightness of my decision.

And then—into the hushed stillness of that early morning—*God* spoke. I heard His answer in my mind as clearly as I'd ever heard an audible voice! Strong. Urgent. Unbelievable. *"Cindy, if you leave, you will not have a testimony."*

I was stunned. My first thought was, *I'm not interested in a testimony! I just want out!* But He spoke again—even more distinct than the first time.

"If you leave, you will not have a testimony. I want to use your husband in the ministry."

It suddenly struck me that I was standing right in the middle of a spine-tingling, hair-raising, profound "God moment"—just Him and me. A living divine exchange with my Savior!

In that split second, a deep, peaceful awareness enveloped me, and I knew something celestial was being birthed. Nothing like this had ever happened to me before—or to anyone else I knew, for that matter.

My anxiety vanished, the weight of dread fell away, and an exciting expectancy began rising in me—expanding, intensifying, soaring higher! My heart flooded with confidence that Jesus was with me! He had *indeed* heard my prayers all along!

Years of discouragement and despair disintegrated at this monumental intersection of hope. I felt like shouting in triumph, but Jesus wasn't finished. He had more words for me!

"I want you to pray and fast until your husband comes to know Me."

Now I realized I stood at a crossroads. I *wanted* to believe God's promises more than anything, but no one would force me to stay in this marriage—not even God.

I faced two options—option 1: continue with *my* plans to leave or option 2: go with *God's* plan and stay.

My whole life hinged on my answer—and the first option seemed most logical.

Let's face it, Cindy, everyone you know has cast their vote. Rick isn't worth fighting for—he's a lost cause. You've got biblical grounds. Give it up! He will never change!

I was so tired of staying in this swamp of a hopeless marriage. I was so tired of hearing those words, "Rick will never change," continually repeated by the people I loved and respected. What if they were right?

But . . . what if they were wrong? What if there *was* a miracle in the making?

Option 2 felt like a huge risk. *Trust what you heard God say, even though you don't know the outcome.* This option came with another equally enormous risk I wasn't sure I was willing to take—I would need to move forward facing *more* years of heartache and disappointments. And deep down, I knew I had *no* forgiveness for Rick. So how would God even make that work?

My thoughts flew back and forth. God had never spoken to me like this before—so sacred and special, beyond anything I'd thought or imagined. I knew I could never explain it away.

So, I stood there in my bathroom, feeling like the tile floor was holy ground. *God, are You really speaking to* me? *Are You really going to give* me *a miracle?*

I felt my heart nudging me to step forward and go all in with Jesus—to abandon myself and take Him at His word.

He had just made a promise directly to me!

For years I said God's promises didn't end with question marks—only periods. This was my moment to show how much I believed those words.

I felt joy and peace spreading across my heart, smoothing away the jagged edges of my questions. I didn't want to miss out on *anything* with God—*especially* a miracle! I *knew* He kept His promises and I was going to *live that belief*, by His grace.

Glancing in the mirror, something was noticeably different. For the first time in years, I saw *real* hope in my eyes. Hope that wouldn't fade away. Hope that would continually run deep and true.

I spoke aloud, "Yes, Lord! I will do it! I will take You at Your word. I will pray *and* fast just as You have asked."

There was no denying I'd heard the voice of God speaking that morning. I wanted to bask in His presence and never leave. This fresh cup of consolation set my heart on fire to go forward in faith!

Pray Big

I *still* had no idea what the future held—or even the details of what I'd agreed to so promptly. But I was more than willing to find out.

I desperately wanted to watch Him work a miracle in my life, and I wanted to be part of *His* plan. I couldn't imagine *how* He was going to do what He said He would do, but I trusted Him.

And I made the commitment to lean on Him wholly.

> Trust in the LORD with all your heart,
> And lean not on your own understanding;
> In all your ways acknowledge Him,
> And He shall direct your paths (Proverbs 3:5, 6).

I want to pause here in my testimony and speak to anyone facing domestic violence or threats of violence. God loves you and He does not call you to stay in an unsafe situation. You can pray from a distance. Even if you feel hopeless, you are not alone. Help is available. For excellent spiritual and professional resources addressing abuse, please visit www.enditnow.org.

Chapter 12

August 6, 2002

Convinced now my prayers were heard, I made the most important appointment of my life—an appointment with God. The vividness of that early Tuesday morning made an everlasting impression.

I will never forget it—ever.

The incessant buzz of the alarm clock woke me at 4:00 A.M. But in stark contrast to the morning before, I arose *eagerly* and quietly made my way to the dining room table. I stopped at the bookcase, picking up my Bible, pen, and highlighter. Next, I added a forty-day prayer journal with inspiring devotionals, I'd recently purchased, to my pile.

The peaceful, serene moments before daybreak provided the perfect opportunity to start something new. My heart bowed low with prayer—both familiar yet fresh.

I *still* hoped (and anticipated) God would use my prayers to change everything for the better—*especially* my husband. But now my heart felt new—without the anxious desperation I usually carried. The promise that He would give me a testimony glowed within me.

Only twenty-four hours before, Determined Cindy had her mind set to walk away from an impossible failed marriage, never to return. But now, Hopeful Cindy was staying—willing to be used by God.

Yet even with this infusion of hope, my courage felt frail. My heart was badly damaged by the pain, bitterness, and exhaustion of our marital warfare.

But as humbly and obediently as I knew how, I placed my fragile heart in Jesus' hands.

Coming to this appointment, I carried two pieces of particularly *heavy* baggage.

First, my flailing prayer and study life—a dramatic boost to my spiritual status was definitely in order. Although I truly loved Jesus, to say I was living as a *committed* believer simply wasn't true.

I thought of friends I considered spiritual saints. They didn't live like I did—as two different people when their surroundings changed. Take my co-worker Dave, for example. I had seen him in a variety of situations, and he didn't just *say* he was a follower of Christ; he *lived* it—all the time. To put it plainly—Dave's talk matched his walk.

I *wanted* to be that person. I *meant* to be that person; I just couldn't get there.

In my spiritual surroundings, I appeared to be faithful and devoted. In my personal life, though, I watched and listened to things I shouldn't, frequently gossiped, cursed, and served up a bitter brew to Rick daily.

Back and forth, I fluctuated between these extremes. Secretly, I felt like a failure. But now I came to my appointment with Jesus and hesitantly laid this shameful burden at His feet.

Please forgive me, Lord, for all the times I came so close to going "all in" with You, only to stop short way too often. I don't want to be indecisive—one person today and a different one tomorrow. I want You to have full custody of my heart.

I carried the second piece of heavy baggage for so many years that even my conversation with God hadn't quite removed the weight. Actually, the weight *did* fall away *in the moment*, but I knew the fearful doubts lurked—ready to spring back strong and vicious.

Simply put, I was afraid I'd worn God out with my unrelenting tears and prayers about our marriage. All I heard in response to my desperate pleadings through the years was "apparent" silence. I knew He still loved me, but the deafening quiet made Him feel distant.

Would this time be different? Clutching my faith, I beat back anxiety with a promise from Isaiah. The beautiful words assured me that the Lord of the universe understood me better than I understood myself. I could *not* wear Him out with my pleas.

> Have you not known?
> Have you not heard?
> The everlasting God, the LORD,
> The Creator of the ends of the earth,
> Neither faints nor is weary.
> His understanding is unsearchable (Isaiah 40:28).

Resting in His love and eager to begin my appointment, I opened my new prayer journal. The first words seemed to jump off the page.

"Have you ever said, 'Lord, something's got to give'?"

Are you kidding me? More than once!

I continued reading and soon added these words in the margin: *There has got to be more to life than this!*

The first chapter of my new forty-day journal brought welcome comfort and encouragement. References to Noah, Elijah, Moses, and Jonah, each spending forty days with God, were interjected in the devotional portion.

I reasoned that if Jesus Himself was led by the Holy Spirit to spend special time with God, I should certainly do the same. Regardless of the outcome with Rick, my time dedicated to seeking God would be time well spent.

HOPE was what I craved—yes, spelled just like that—in all capital letters. A tiny crumb from the Master's table was all I needed; just a little word from Jesus, along with His illuminating light to shine into the dark recesses of my heart.

Thankfully, Jesus, God's Word, and the journal were filling my desolate spaces. "Now may the God of hope fill you with all joy and peace in believing, that you may abound in hope by the power of the Holy Spirit" (Romans 15:13).

Merriam-Webster's Collegiate Dictionary defines *hope* as "to cherish a desire with anticipation, to want something to happen or be true."[1]

What a perfect definition! I was expecting *great things* from a *great God!*

Next, an application section of the journal brought me up short again.

I had been sailing along in my comfort zone as I read. But now, I was being asked to respond and go deeper. Yikes!

Am I ready for this?

What will I do if I hear things from You that I don't want to hear, God?

What if real prayer isn't all wrapped up in a pretty package? I don't know what to do if it turns out messy and complicated.

The exercise began with Matthew 6:33, "But seek first the kingdom of God and His righteousness, and all these things shall be added to you."

A barrage of questions came next:

"Is Jesus your first love?" *"Yes!"* I wrote.

"Have you repented and surrendered *all* to Jesus and asked Him to be Lord of your life?" *"I know I have failed to ask for forgiveness in the past when You wanted obedience from me."* Not to mention the overwhelming guilt that burdened me. My efforts to abide in Him were pitiful. My life was one big mess. If *only* I could surrender fully.

I looked down, absolutely speechless at my answers to these and other questions. I *believed* that He was my first love, but my heart and other journal entries revealed a *much* different scenario. Regrettably, Jesus was second place in *most* areas of my life—even *last* place in some.

I knew a *lot* of Bible stories and a *lot* of things *about* Jesus, but to say He was my first love would be incorrect. I loved Rick passionately and the life he once offered me. The love for my boys was unfathomable, but that was because I *knew* them and spent a lot of time with them. Jesus was barely given a passing glance the majority of my young adult life.

I prayerfully reviewed the suggestions on making Jesus first in my life, knowing they applied to me.

The final question, seeming more like a riddle, beckoned an answer.

"What is His will for your life?" I desperately wanted to know. With pen in hand, I wrote, *"Everything You say, I will do, Lord."* Then I read Psalm 27:8, "When You said, 'Seek My face,' my heart said to You, 'Your face, Lord, I will seek.' "

I wasn't sure of the correct response, but I was certain of the solution. Seeking Him was the *only* option. Nothing else really mattered anymore.

The author strongly recommended seeking the things of God more than seeking things that *Cindy* desired during the upcoming forty-day period. She ended with one more question:

"What do you desire most for yourself?" That response came easily: *"For me and my family to have a solid foundation to stand the test of time until the Lord returns."*

I suppose that wasn't a bad way to answer that question. And I prayed wholeheartedly for the courage to remain steadfast in my quest to follow Him this time.

August 6, 2002

Lord, this is very new and different for me—an area of my spiritual walk that should have been birthed years ago. I am guilty of abandoning this wonderful journey. I will seek You and find You—for that is what You have promised.

What are Your plans for me? Please reveal them to me through Your discerning Holy Spirit. Discipline me to stand in the gap for everyone on my prayer list and all those that You prompt me to pray for. Help me get cleaned up—so that I can intercede for others so that they can one day share this experience with You.

I love You, Lord.

Stay my first love and my first priority.

---

1. *Merriam-Webster's Collegiate Dictionary*, 11th ed. (Springfield, MA: Merriam-Webster, 2003), s.v. "hope."

Chapter 13

When God first spoke to me in my despair, asking me to stay and *pray* for Rick, I felt I could handle *that* request. However, His additional instruction to *fast* concerned me greatly.

At first, I glossed over it, thinking it was just formality. After all, those two words—*fast* and *pray*—often went together in spiritual conversations. *Surely,* they weren't to be taken literally.

But on day 2 of my reflection time, the topic resurfaced.

Very few people in my faith circle discussed fasting, so I wasn't familiar with the practice. But I did know two things about it thanks to Momma and the Baptist church of my childhood.

I was eleven years old when Brother Hoven made an announcement one Sunday morning that the upcoming week would include an opportunity for dedicated fasting days. All who desired to participate made a private commitment with God.

On the ride home from church, Momma explained that fasting meant not eating. She went on to explain she'd spend extra time praying about the things on her heart.

Later that week, during her fast, I noticed quiet tears on her face. Twirling my hair around my finger in worry, I asked, "Why are you crying, Momma?"

"Oh, it's nothing, Cindy."

I kept staring at her knowing it was *something*.

"I'll be fine, don't you worry," she added. "It's not a bad thing—it's a good thing—really. Sometimes I cry when I'm praying because I feel closer to God."

I believed her even though I didn't understand.

Now, as I contemplated entering the mysteries of fasting myself, all I could picture was no food *and* crying. Neither was appealing to me.

But Momma's words still stood out in my mind—*"I feel closer to God."*

One thing was very clear. God was calling me to pray *and* fast until I was close enough to Him to *believe* He could actually do what He said He would do.

Soon, I found more confirmation about the crucial need for fasting. "So He said to them, 'This kind can come out by nothing but prayer and fasting' " (Mark 9:29).

When Jesus made the statement in Mark 9:29, "This kind can come out by nothing but prayer and fasting," He was talking about *this kind* of *unbelief.* I needed to pray and fast until I was fully persuaded that God could do everything He promised me He would do.

Unsure of how to proceed, I optimistically petitioned God day after day for answers. As I moved forward on my knees, He gradually impressed me to plan for three days of dedicated fasting and prayer.

While continuing my search for answers, I closely guarded my special time with Jesus. I felt sure my new commitment would be strongly challenged, but Determined Cindy refused to let God's promise of a miracle slip away.

On day 9 of my early morning prayer time, I got quite an unwelcomed jolt. "Check Your Heart" was the topic in my prayer journal that day.

My heart is fine, God! I mean, I don't like *the things Rick has done, but I'll move past the hurt—eventually.*

Deep inside, I knew these words were hollow. I could fool plenty of people, but there was no fooling myself or God.

My heart for Rick needed *major* work.

This is great—just great, I thought sourly. *I still haven't figured out the fasting issue, and now I have another problem to deal with somehow.*

Since I was a "stuffer," cramming everything down inside, I never dealt with the painful emotions from many of our marriage issues. Instead, they festered and flourished under the surface. Plain and simple, a lack of forgiveness now rooted *deeply* in my heart.

The enemy reminded me constantly of *all* the pain I'd endured—and *kept* enduring! Over and over! Just when I thought I'd somehow managed to move past the hurt and forgive Rick yet again, something *else* would happen—guaranteed.

The wound *never* healed. Forgiving my husband was the absolute *last* item on my to-do list—down at the very bottom where I didn't even have to look at it.

Now words from the first day of my forty-day study kept ringing in my ear: *Something's got to give. Something's got to give.*

I suspected, uncomfortably, that one of those "somethings" was my cold, stony heart—calcified and hardened with pain, gossip, and anger at Rick. *I have a right to a cold, stony heart—don't be ridiculous! After all, look at all I've been through.*

But as justified as I felt, I also experienced unease. Over the past few months, I'd sensed Jesus whispering, *"Go ahead, Cindy, give Me all your years of pain and heartaches. You weren't designed to carry this load. I'll help you every step of the way. It's OK to tell Me exactly what's in your heart."*

However, I resisted it. Being honest with God about *everything* seemed virtually impossible—and now I needed to understand why I felt this way. I knew that until I could trust Him *with everything*, my cold heart would never be warm.

I discovered I had an inaccurate picture of Jesus that kept me from expressing my true feelings to Him. For one thing, I perceived Him as unapproachable—or too busy for me.

Surely prayer wasn't a place to unload all my stored-up sarcasm—to starkly verbalize my deep hurts and burning anger toward my husband. What would God think of me? Certainly, I'd fall in His esteem if I let loose with all the ugliness inside.

But as the days passed, my precious early mornings with Jesus opened my eyes to see that these impressions were distorted and untrue. I didn't need polite phrases when I talked with Him. He truly *wanted* every last burden I carried, no matter how deep or ugly. "Therefore humble yourselves under the mighty hand of God, that He may exalt you in due time, casting all your care upon Him, for He cares for you" (1 Peter 5:6, 7).

God Can Do So Much More

I pushed forward with processing my honest emotions before God. But now the ugly cauldron of bitter stew was out in the open, and it wasn't pretty. As much as I tried to dismiss it, I could not get rid of the detestable monster making me miserable.

While I struggled through what forgiveness looked like, God sent more help at my midweek Bible-study group. One evening as everyone gathered, I was chatting with my good friend Alicia (who also happened to be Rick's cousin). She was excited about a new book she'd just read and quickly pulled it out to show me.

The title was *Total Forgiveness!*

Seriously! How could Alicia know that I am struggling with that very thing? I wondered. *God, did You tell her to bring this book to me?*

She held it out. "Would you like to read it, Cindy?"

"Hmm, yes, I would *love* to read it! Thanks, Alicia."

Our lesson study was beginning, but I couldn't keep my mind off the book in my purse. I wanted to leave church right then and start reading.

Arriving home, I hurriedly finished my chores and crawled into bed with my new book. I made it through two forewords, the preface, the intriguing introduction, and well into chapter 1 when it happened.

Drip, drip, sniffle, drip, drip, sniffle.

No matter how hard I tried to hold back my tears, they fell fast. Multiple wet spots now accompanied the yellow highlighter marks adorning the pages. Thankfully, the book was mine to keep.

My unexpected, overflowing emotions confirmed my bitter, hard-hearted condition. With deep gratefulness, I added this book to my daily feast of prayer, Scripture, and journaling.

By now, my preparations for a three-day fast were complete, and the anticipated day arrived. Ready or not, I took the leap to begin this strange exercise. I felt lost and out of sorts.

What will I do without food? Starve and cry seemed like fitting options. *That should work well at the surgery center.*

With my water bottle and Bible in hand, I made my way to the car.

What are you doing, Cindy? I continued my pessimistic monologue. *You won't even make it through the first day, much less three days!*

But something happened once my car wheels hit the highway. First, I firmly put aside my sour forebodings. Then I enthusiastically verbalized out loud, "Good morning, God, good morning Son, good morning Holy Spirit!"

Realizing my radio was tuned into a secular station, I turned it off. The lyrics coming out of the speaker didn't align with the sacred, serious dialogue I'd begun with God that morning. *There, much better*, I sighed.

Our conversation grew more spirited and uplifting. *I can do this through You, Lord!* And, *You really* are *going to change my husband, aren't You, God?*

The rest of the drive passed way too quickly. It was just me and Jesus— undisturbed by the world outside. He talked, I listened. I talked, He listened. We had a perfect prayer conversation.

Normally at work, I started the day by preparing for the first surgery case, then headed to the break room. Today, when I walked in, my eyes immediately flew to the tempting platters of doughnuts, yummy pastries, cereal of all kinds, and the variety of bagels laid out in a generous smorgasbord. Chattering voices and morning headlines blaring from the TV filled the room with constant babble.

This certainly isn't going to fit into my new fasting schedule, God! I didn't think about all the distractions I would face.

Thankfully, I was able to escape and find a quiet place for my thoughts, prayer time, and Bible reading before the busy day commenced.

That first day of fasting was *really* hard. My stomach made loud, obnoxious sounds, and I was starving by 9:00 A.M. For the first time, I wondered if I'd misunderstood God's voice regarding fasting.

Am I doing this right, God? Am I supposed to feel horrible?

My circulator duties in the operating room required careful concentration. However, after the surgeon made the incision, I was usually free to begin the necessary paperwork for the surgery case. This time gave me a small window of opportunity to silently talk with Jesus.

Our "talks" began with me praising God for His greatness and transitioned to my long list of requests—especially for Rick to change. Of course, I included others in my prayers, but 95 percent of the pleas were for my husband. The loathsome list was a broken record.

Please, Lord, give Rick the desire to stop smoking and drinking. Give him a hatred for drugs and pornography. Help him turn to You and be the husband I know You want him to be.

I prayed this prayer day in and day out for years. *How long, Lord? How much longer?*

But now, fasting added a new dimension. Every time my tummy rumbled, I prayed my prayer for Rick yet again.

During breaks, I read my Bible and prayed the prayer some more. On the ride home, I kept praying. *Every* available moment was spent saturating my mind with prayer and encouraging Scripture.

Even though I still had no idea what I was doing, I marched on with my total food fast, making sure to drink plenty of liquids. The second day was much better.

Soon, a small "spring" developed in my step, accompanied by a growing positive outlook. As the third day rolled around, I was definitely hungry, but increasing the fluids helped quiet my growling tummy.

I kept giving God my best and trusting Him for wisdom.

To my delight and surprise, some wonderful, unexpected benefits occurred. My mind was super clear, and my ear was tuned to God's voice more than ever! Familiar verses now held deeper significance.

At certain moments, it seemed angels bent low and whispered, *You are not alone—we are with you.* And I remembered Momma's words about fasting, *"I feel closer to God."*

On the afternoon of the third day, I arrived home and immediately noticed something odd. There were more unopened beer cans than usual remaining in the carton.

Well, isn't that interesting. Rick didn't drink as many beers today! I raised my eyebrows and thanked God for this small but significant surprise that encouraged me in my fasting obedience.

Day by day, I sensed Him increasing my faith, and I wanted more—*lots* more. Despite my original fear, I didn't starve. Instead, I felt good—*really* good.

With my first fasting experience now over, I eagerly awaited God's prompting to begin another. But I soon discovered He had something different in mind for my next step.

Chapter 14

Several weeks had passed since that morning when I'd been ready to leave my marriage forever. But instead, God spoke directly to my heart. His amazing promise to give me a testimony if I would hang in and trust Him only glowed more strongly as my faith grew.

Rick, of course, knew nothing of that crossroads—or how God showed me more about Himself every day. Outwardly, our life continued much as it had before.

Rick worked hard and provided for us very well financially. He was still the great father he'd always been. But he also continued to be as emotionally distant from me as usual—except when anger reared during the stressful days when he drank too much. *That* dreaded cycle was as predictable as ever.

Surely, any day now, God would begin to fulfill His promise, and Rick would start changing dramatically before my very eyes!

Still, the days dragged on. Eventually, it occurred to me that perhaps I could help speed up the process by sharing the spiritual insights I knew.

After all, who understood better than I how much Rick lived in opposition to God's plan for his life—*plus* how much he truly wanted to change? He just didn't know how, and I was ready and willing to take on the job of sharing *all* my knowledge to help him right along.

Naturally, I tailored my suggestions and comments strategically—speaking at *just* the right moments to best transform his thinking and behavior. I felt blissfully confident that God would look favorably on my aid in turning my husband's heart to Him.

However, my self-appointed position as Rick's chief conviction officer (CCO) didn't go *nearly* as smoothly as I'd envisioned. Nor did it accomplish the desired outcome.

My attempts to persuade and influence not only failed but they also created *more* barriers between us (which, frankly, I hadn't even thought possible).

Nevertheless, I kept plowing ahead. I couldn't yet see how my "repeated exhortations" were actually harsh nagging; my "firm commitment to point out truth," was really a prideful determination to always have the last word.

Without even realizing it, I tried to take the place of the Holy Spirit. My number one priority was to *change* Rick—but everything I tried failed *miserably*.

Plus, it drained me physically and emotionally.

In addition to diligently striving in my CCO position, I still struggled with anger and resentment for *all* the times Rick hurt me. I felt he *deserved* to be apprised of his failings and never hesitated to inflict guilt trips on him. I wanted to somehow *get justice* by making *him* feel as bad as he made *me* feel.

Often I met him at the door with a series of rapid-fire questions: "Do you know what time it is? Where have you been? Don't you care about us?" And, of course, my favorite, "Do you realize how many beers you drank today?"

Nothing improved. My despair grew as I realized Rick wasn't changing *at all*, no matter *what* I tried. My cajoling words had no effect—and my wounding words only created more chaos.

Frustration welled higher in me every day. I *wanted* to hurry up and forgive him, but he needed to change *first*! He needed to *apologize* and *assure* me by his actions that my forgiveness wouldn't be wasted.

I vacillated between a genuine longing for him to experience the peace of Jesus and resenting that he wouldn't change, thereby making my life miserable—plus depriving me of the chance to forgive him once he reformed.

My heart toward Rick was one big, mixed-up mess.

But now, instead of stuffing it all down inside as I had for years, I began pouring it out to God in my precious early morning prayer time.

What am I going to do about this, God? You told me You want to use Rick in ministry—but he's not changing. And, apparently, You're going to have to do some-thing about me too! My heart's in no condition to be the wife of someone in ministry!

The answers didn't come. I kept praying—and praying—and struggling—and praying—day after day—week after week.

One morning, in desperation, I slipped out of my chair to kneel brokenly before God.

What is it You want, Lord? I'm releasing everything to You that I know how to do! Is there something You want to tell me? I'm listening; please speak to me!

But I heard nothing from God—just silence. My tears started spilling as I pressed on.

Lord, I know my heart is hard, and You know it better than I. I've really tried to get past this, but it's so difficult. I'm tired of avoiding the issue. So—go ahead, take it—it's Yours anyway. You *are the true desire of my heart. Here,* I held my hands over my heart, looking toward heaven, *take my stone-cold heart, once and for all, and exchange it for a heart of flesh filled with forgiveness. Take away my selfish, self-righteous spirit, and give me Your Spirit.*

Almost instantaneously, I felt something warm and light flooding through my heart. My calloused resistance suddenly cracked and broke under the unstoppable power of His love.

My next words flowed out with my tears, taking me by complete surprise. *Lord, please give my husband a new wife—and let it be me.*

With God's presence hovering over me (and floods of tears), I symbolically placed my foot in the Jordan River to begin a forgiveness journey that morning. I knew God would carry me through the days and weeks ahead—all the way to victory.

In that transforming moment, my prayer expanded radically—beyond anything I could ever imagine. For years, I prayed Rick would become a new husband to *me*. Now, I was also praying *he* would have a new wife.

Without excusing or overlooking my husband's own struggles, I realized the battle ahead was no longer about Rick Mercer—it was about *me* trust-ing God to fulfill *His* promise in *His* timing. A new wave of determination washed over me as I joyfully resigned from my CCO position.

By eliminating my own agenda, more room opened in my heart for the Holy Spirit. I pledged to spend less time focusing on Rick's lack of conviction and more time invested in receiving my own.

But I knew stepping back from trying to manage Rick's conversion was easy compared to the *real* battle I faced. My *far greater hurdle* was forgiving him—because it felt like *letting go*: letting go of justice and letting go of the walls in my heart I'd built to protect against pain.

Although I was more than ready for God to remove the years of bitterness from my heart, I also felt afraid. Forgiveness meant risking everything.

Forgiveness feels like the hardest thing to do, God—to let go of the hurt and trust that You are big enough to heal.

I don't see how You can do that. But my heart is Yours.

Relinquishing layers of stuff, accumulated through years of pain, seemed far-fetched and impossible. If only Rick would change *first*. If he would make *efforts* and *apologize* and *acknowledge* how much he'd wronged me—*then* I might be able to find a desire to forgive.

But now, I felt the Holy Spirit calling me to look higher—in new directions entirely. During my devotional times with Jesus, I dived into the book about forgiveness from Alicia. One morning I read Colossians 3:13, "Bearing with one another, and forgiving one another, if anyone has a complaint against another; even as Christ forgave you, so you also must do."

That certainly sounded nice in theory. After all, I was more than grateful for the undeserved grace and forgiveness God had given *me*!

But for me to extend this same kind of gift to *Rick* was a completely different story. How could I *do* that? God *knew* all I'd been through! It was impossible!

I continued reading, praying, and pouring out every last painful, angry memory to God. Gradually, I felt little glimmers of a miracle dawning in my heart. The heavy, built-up grudges deep down inside, the finger-pointing, the wanting justification for my pain—all began slowly melting away as I discovered Him calling me to lay it aside forever.

I learned I'd been fighting a war I could never win—because my husband wasn't the real enemy. "For we do not wrestle against flesh and blood, but against principalities, against powers, against the rulers of the darkness of this age, against spiritual hosts of wickedness in the heavenly places" (Ephesians 6:12).

Only God could win the battle against the true enemy. And *He* was fighting *for* me.

As the Holy Spirit opened my eyes to see through new lenses, the fight to forgive didn't seem so hard anymore. I discovered the beautiful truth that forgiveness didn't require Rick to meet *my* expectations.

True forgiveness happened when I set my expectations and my confidence in God—not in Rick or anyone else for that matter.

This miraculous sense of freedom grew stronger and clearer in my heart as time passed. One day, I felt astonished to realize I'd lost my fixation on whether Rick was even changing. It simply wasn't on my radar anymore.

The more the King of the universe set up residence in my heart, the more I learned the road to forgiveness was a process—not once and done, but decision by decision, moment by moment.

Over time, I noticed His instruction changed not only my inner thoughts but my outward behavior. The words coming out of my mouth became dramatically different. This noticeable softening of my speech actually surprised *me*.

Instead of letting Rick know all the ways he disappointed me, I'd find something positive to say instead. "I appreciate your help today." Or, "Thanks for cooking dinner tonight, that helped out a lot!"

Other times, I discovered it was best if I said nothing at all, not in the sense of a punishing session of "silent treatment" but in the sense of being gracious and simply not saying certain things. It was amazing how my patient silence could change the environment in a peaceful way—even when I felt what I desperately wanted to say was true!

I also stopped venting to my mom and close friends about Rick's failures. I knew this only built walls between these people and Rick.

Now that Jesus was tearing down the walls in my heart, I *certainly* didn't want to be putting them up for anyone else. Plus, with Jesus as my Protector, I didn't need the temporary comfort of their sympathetic validation anymore.

At first, this awkward adaptation to curtail my sarcastic observations and cultivate a heart of forgiveness wasn't easy. Not at all! Sometimes the stinging phrases dangled by a thread on the tip of my tongue almost *begging* to be said.

However, I'd made a commitment to God—giving Him full permission to change my heart. Thankfully, the Holy Spirit continued the much-needed alterations in me, just as Philippians 1:6 promised. *You can be confident, Cindy, of this very thing—that He who has begun this good work in you will complete it.*

Months passed, and I joyfully recorded in my prayer journal that I could actually *see* positive strides in our conversations! What a marvelous milestone in my prayer journey, to be sure!

God Can Do So Much More

Another beautiful truth God showed me during this time was how to use His promises when I was tempted to give in to hurt or anger.

Two powerful verses became the bedrock of my prayer life.

"Now to Him who is able to do exceedingly abundantly above all that we ask or think, according to the power that works in us" (Ephesians 3:20).

"Call to Me, and I will answer you, and show you great and mighty things, which you do not know" (Jeremiah 33:3).

Both were easy to memorize and personalize, so I repeated them often out loud as I drove to work or cleaned the house. At work, I repeated them silently as I transported patients down the hall to the surgery suite.

Cindy, call out to Me. I hear you, and I will answer you. Great things are coming. I will show you.

The more I focused on God's powerful promises, the less I focused on the problems. His promises became bigger—and my problems became smaller.

Lord, I'm so happy with the changes in my heart! I feel like I can breathe again. Thank You for never leaving my side. I'm so thankful for the small changes in Rick, but I know there is more—because You promised. Please keep me from growing weary. Help me stay faithful to Your Word and follow You completely.

I once read a story about Florence Chadwick. She was a champion swimmer—the first woman to swim the English Channel in both directions.

In 1952, she set another personal goal—to swim twenty-six miles from Catalina Island to the coast of California. Her most significant barrier to completing the swim was not the distance but the freezing-cold temperatures of the Pacific Ocean. In addition, fog often rolled in without warning—so thick she could only see inches in front of her.

On the appointed day, Florence swam for *fifteen hours* through the bone-chilling waters and grey fog. But finally, overcome, she gave up. She hadn't known she was less than a half mile from shore. Though not one for making excuses, Florence knew that *seeing* land ahead would have given her the extra push she needed to make it the final distance.

Sometime later, she decided to try again, hoping for a different outcome. Yet again, the fog drifted in and obscured her ability to see her destination.

However, *this* time, she kept swimming. She kept reminding herself that land was there and within her reach!

Confident in what she *knew* in her heart to be true even though she could not *see* it, she bravely swam to victory—breaking the record by two hours![1]

This amazing story provides so much hope in the journey of forgiveness!

There was definitely "fog" in the process—days when things didn't go well, days when past hurts and fresh pain all rolled together to discourage the work the Holy Spirit was doing in me.

But I kept reminding myself, *The fog will clear, the land is ahead!*

Like Florence, I had a goal—a prayer goal. God's promise offered hope.

His words assured me that beyond the pain and struggle to forgive, in His strength, it could happen! Trusting Him as my Guide, I confidently kept praying.

I could almost hear Jesus coaching in my ear, *"Pray, Cindy, pray! Keep going—you're going to make it!"* "Rejoicing in hope, patient in tribulation, continuing steadfastly in prayer" (Romans 12:12).

---

1. Channel Swimming Association Ltd., "Florence Chadwick 1953–1964," Queen of the Channel, https://www.queenofthechannel.com/florence-chadwick.

Chapter 15

December 2002 arrived, and although my forty-day prayer journey was complete, I had no intention of stopping there! This was just the beginning of a glorious launch toward spiritual wholeness.

I treasured my lifelines of daily prayer and studying God's Word, and occasional times of fasting, which elevated me to healing heights. Yoking up with Jesus through these vital components changed everything!

Yes, short-lived valleys of despair persisted, but the canyons didn't seem as deep. My heart waited quietly on the promise as I actively cultivated a life that offered something more.

And always, a reassuring quote or scripture came my way just when I needed it most.

The holiday season was full of hustle and bustle, including major plans in full swing for the annual Christmas party hosted by the surgery department. The anticipated affair required weeks of preparation in order to provide the perfect evening.

We had attended the exciting festivities for the past four years, and Rick readily jumped at the chance to "play" bartender when asked. He wasn't interested in the nice food or music—only in making mixed drinks for everyone— which included helping himself to a few.

As an added "benefit," he took home the leftover alcohol from the party. At the end of the night, he carried out armfuls of beer and hard liquor as his esteemed prize for his bartending service.

In the past, I enjoyed this yearly celebration with my coworkers and their companions. But my interest in attending the party waned dramatically this year in light of my current walk with Christ.

However, employees were "expected" to at least make an appearance for dinner. With only a few weeks remaining before the big event, I reluctantly jumped into planning mode with everyone at work.

When the night of the gala came around, and we arrived at the party, I promptly walked to the kitchen to help with last-minute meal preparations. As expected, Rick went straight to the bar to prepare the inventory of alcohol for the guests.

With my kitchen duties complete, I engaged in conversation with some friends while Rick continued to "taste test" his concoctions. Finishing my small talk with the girls, I turned to walk toward Rick and stopped dead in my tracks.

I couldn't believe what I was seeing! Rick was talking to *Dave*!

I wonder what they're talking about! My curiosity skyrocketed.

As I stood in the candlelit banquet room, watching in awe, a feeling of soft warmth covered me. All at once, the scene transitioned into a seemingly slow-motion picture.

Dear Lord, could Dave be the one to lead him to You?

The impression lodged in my heart strongly. After all, Dave *had* been praying for Rick for quite some time.

Apparently, Dave didn't just pray for people; he *actively* built connections. On this night, he deliberately sought out Rick to talk with him. I knew Dave didn't drink alcohol, but he'd crossed to the separate area of the bar and stood there visiting with my husband.

What are You up to, Lord?

After what seemed like forever, their conversation concluded with Dave giving a friendly nod to me as he walked back over to join his wife, Lisa, for dinner. I cautiously approached Rick, noticing he appeared to be deep in thought.

With his eyes still on Dave, Rick gave a slight shake of his head. "There's something different about that guy," he said half to himself.

"Yes, there is," I smiled. "He's a Christian!"

"Well, I can tell. That guy is *real*. He wasn't fake—he's genuine," he replied. This was some of the highest praise Rick could give. He turned thoughtfully to resume stocking the bar for the evening ahead.

Since Rick wasn't hungry, I joined my coworkers at the beautifully decorated tables adorned with fresh evergreens and flickering candles. The meal was delicious, and soon the DJ pumped up the volume on the tunes, indicating it was dance time.

Dave and Lisa politely excused themselves from the evening activities at this point. As I watched them slip out the door, I suddenly recalled an earlier profound encounter between Rick and Dave.

Months earlier, Rick's oldest son needed hernia surgery, which made my husband very nervous. He couldn't bear the thought of his child being cut on, much less being put to sleep under general anesthesia.

Knowing Dave already had our names in his prayer book, and that he customarily prayed for his patients, I requested that he pray for Farron's procedure. Admittedly, it was a long shot because of scheduling and availability conflicts for fifteen anesthesia personnel. Dr. Samuel assured me he'd try.

My motive in asking for Dave was twofold: his skills were commendable, *and* I hoped God would set up a divine appointment through Dave's expected prayers for Farron.

The morning of the surgery came. When Dave popped in the room with his bright, beaming smile, my heart rejoiced in gratitude. *Thank You, Lord—another prayer answered!*

After a cheery good morning and some small talk, Dave began the preprocedural interview and concluded with a pat on Farron's shoulder. Now he switched the conversation smoothly just as expected.

"Well, hey, how about prayer for this guy! Would that be OK with everyone?" he asked.

The moment felt surreal. For over seven years, I watched Dave offer a prayer for *thousands* of patients. Now it was *our* turn.

"Absolutely, we would love that!" Rick answered.

This is good, God, this is really good, I rejoiced, followed by an imaginary high five to God with a huge smile on my face!

Once the comforting plea was offered to heaven and the amen said, we thanked Dave for helping alleviate our fears. Then he turned to Farron. "You ready, bud?" With a nod to the family, Dave and the nurse transported him down the hall to the operating room.

After they left, I surveyed the calm, assured faces around me. It seemed we all felt that Farron was indeed in good hands.

Rick broke the silence. "That doctor was *really* nice to pray for my son like that."

"That wasn't the doctor, that was Dave," I answered with a smile. "He's the nurse anesthetist, and he'll be putting Farron to sleep and waking him up."

And he's the one that's been praying for you *for months now—he'll probably even pray for you in a few minutes after Farron is asleep*, I mused silently.

I believed this interaction was no coincidence. God was up to something—and once again, prayer was the conduit.

Lord, You never cease to amaze me. I can't wait to see more!

Now a voice pulled me starkly back to the present.

"Cindy—Cindy, hey, are you listening to me? Girl, where's your mind? Are you going to eat or just hold that fork? Hurry up; it's time to dance!" My attention returned to the Christmas party, the flickering candles, and the laughing conversations around the room.

Hours later, the long evening ended with "Auld Lang Syne" playing while we cleaned up. As predicted, we walked out with a surplus of unopened alcohol. Rick was happily buzzed, so I hopped in the driver's seat, anxious to get home.

Just as I approached the parking lot exit, I got my second shock of the evening. Into the silence, Rick made a random comment that stunned me.

"Who knows—I might not even be drinking this time next year," he said, gazing out the window into the starry Arkansas sky.

An audible *Hmm* quietly escaped my lips as I pulled onto the highway and headed south. *All I can say, Lord, is* that *would be a miracle!*

Panoramas of the evening continued to play through my mind—especially Rick and Dave's interaction and Rick's unusual comments. *Maybe Dave really is the one after all!*

Our drive home was quiet, and the rest of the Christmas season was mostly enjoyable. So much had changed in the last twelve months, and I wondered what the New Year might bring.

Chapter 16

One night, I sat at my computer with my finger hovering over the Enter key. I was about to make a *huge* purchase on eBay.

Although I'd achieved my career dream of being a nurse, I also held an unrelenting desire to do something additional that was fun and creative. Idle time wasn't in my vocabulary, so I reasoned an exciting business venture was just what the doctor ordered to soothe away my stress. I scanned the internet daily, looking for the perfect unique hobby.

After much research and prayer, my hunt was over. Selling shaved ice was the winner!

To avoid going overboard, I opted for a nice, gently used industrial ice shaver. The price was fair but not cheap.

Originally, I planned on starting small with just a few supplies and one shaving machine. However, the more I salivated over the possibilities, the bigger my vision grew.

Several nights later, I discovered a *new* listing fitting my vision perfectly! Multiple pictures showcasing a shaved ice trailer sent me into orbit. Not only did it come with a practically new industrial shaver, the owner was including all the mixing bottles and extra tools too. I immediately sent a message to the seller asking for an appointment to see this deluxe refreshment stand on wheels.

Rick and the boys were thrilled about the idea! He encouraged me to pursue the dream and was highly supportive throughout the entire process.

Pray Big

Perfect—one small, family business coming right up!
I wondered why I hadn't thought of it before.

Rick and I made the happy journey together to purchase our new little business. The moment my eyes landed on the shaved ice trailer, I began to squeal!

The equipment was in mint condition and came fully stocked to start the business. My mind overflowed with visions of sweet-tasting flavors in rainbow colors lining the shelves inside.

We agreed upon a price, and away we went—the proud owners of a new shaved ice business. I named it The Iceback Sno-Shack.

Hours upon hours were spent getting everything ready for opening day. Rick eagerly took care of the technical items, arranging for water and electrical hookups, plus purchasing a special freezer for the ice molds. My heart felt light with the fun of working together in tandem with him again.

We signed a contract with a nationally known shaved-ice flavor distributor and attached a colorful new sign on the building. Everything came together superfast, and midmorning, Friday, July 4th, 2003, The Iceback Sno-Shack was open for business in our front yard.

The day was going really well despite my lack of sleep from all the preparations. I had a blast shaving ice and adding the tasty flavors with toppings, and I absolutely loved the big smiles as customers took their first taste.

Family and friends pitched in to help, making our grand opening easier and even *more* fun. My parents traveled over for the big day too. Vehicles filtered in and out throughout the day, and I was overjoyed at the community support.

I accepted the fact we wouldn't make any money that day because every time I turned around, the boys showed up at the serving window, batting their puppy-dog eyes, saying, "Just one more—*please*, Mom!" And who could resist *that*?

Halfway through the day, we'd all enjoyed our share of tutti-frutti, sour apple, sno-ice cream, and many more!

God Can Do So Much More

Rick split his time between chores in the chicken houses and helping me when needed. Sometime after lunch, he excused himself to go purchase steaks, potatoes, and all the fixings for our evening meal. He wanted everything to be special for the big day, plus he loved grilling.

Because of the steady stream of customers, I hardly noticed his return home *or* his occasional entrance into the trailer, as he helped himself to different fruity flavors. Unbeknownst to me, while out getting groceries, he'd also purchased a variety of liquors, including rum, vodka, tequila, and gin. He set up his own little minibar and experimented with different combinations of my shaved-ice flavors.

I was too busy to clue into what was happening, but as the evening drew on, I noticed a drastic change in his behavior. As his attitude and demeanor deteriorated, I grew increasingly concerned. His behavior irritated me greatly, especially with my parents and the boys around—not to mention the last few customers.

A quick, last-minute sale concluded the day just in the nick of time. A refreshing heat shower began to fall on my bare arms as I locked up the Sno-Shack door. The day had been productive, and the future possibilities delighted me.

Rick's sister, Donna, and her husband, Mack, drove up about that time to join us for dinner. The boys impatiently waited for food *and* fireworks.

Oh, fireworks, I thought with an inward groan. *I'm so tired. Maybe they'll forget about it after they eat.*

My feet ached, and I was starving. *Maybe I can sit down for a few minutes and relax before dinner.* Mom and Rick were supposed to be finishing up meal preparations, but as I neared the carport, my heart sank as I heard elevated voices. A heated argument between them escalated quickly. By their exchange of words, I could tell my husband's drinking was the subject matter. It wasn't the first time they'd got into it about Rick's alcohol consumption, so honestly, I wasn't surprised.

She was letting him know he'd pushed his limits for the day, and he wasn't happy with her opinion. By the time I approached them, Dad was involved too.

Thankfully, Donna had already scooted the boys into the house before the unsightly scene began to brew.

Great, just great! Are you kidding me? An argument is the last thing I want to see. My perfect day destroyed! Moving quickly, I mentally switched my "hat" from shaved-ice queen to referee.

Mack was doing his best to diffuse the argument while I screamed at them to stop the nonsense.

But no one seemed to notice me yelling—*or* leaving.

Completely disgusted and at the end of my rope, I turned and started running down our driveway toward the highway. By the time I reached the pavement, uncontrollable sobbing had overtaken me.

With no idea where I was going or what I was doing, I kept running—running from the madness, running from the pain, just running away.

Suddenly, I saw the bright security night light of my small Methodist church and turned in that direction. The rain intensified and began to saturate my clothes and hair.

My pace picked up as I approached the front door of the church. I grabbed the doorknob and was shocked when the door swung open!

The eerie quietness of the sanctuary engulfed me as I stepped inside. I moved to the front and collapsed in exhaustion at the altar. Within minutes, my rapid gasps for air slowed in harmony with my declining heartbeat.

Eventually, my eyes acclimated to the darkness with the help of a small light shining through the small stained-glass window. I remained in an exhausted heap for well over an hour, crying out to God in prayer.

Dear Lord, why did all this happen tonight? I thought things were going smoother with Rick. I guess I shouldn't be shocked by this bump in the road. You've seen me through some major valleys, and I know You'll carry me through this one too.

I certainly hadn't expected this big flare-up between my parents and Rick—stirring the pot on past family tensions. We had been through so much, and I just wanted everyone to get along. Unfortunately, I didn't see that happening anytime soon.

Yet the scriptures I'd read all these months in my morning prayer time came stealing into my heart to bring comfort. I reminded myself the battle belonged to the Lord. *He* would fight for me.

I know You haven't forgotten me, Lord, or Your promise. I'm so tired and frustrated, but I still trust You and Your plans for Rick and me.

The righteous cry out, and the Lord hears,
And delivers them out of all their troubles.

God Can Do So Much More

The LORD is near to those who have a broken heart,
And saves such as have a contrite spirit (Psalm 34:17, 18).

Reluctant to return home, I finally slipped out of the church, still amazed the door was unlocked. My walk home wasn't far, but it felt like forever to get there.

Unsure of what to expect, my feet dragged slowly down the driveway. Immediately, I noticed the absence of my parents' vehicle. They had obviously left. Only Mack and Donna's Silverado pickup truck remained.

Hesitantly walking up the stairs to the back door, I slipped quietly into the house.

As I tiptoed down the hall leading to the living room, I heard Mack, Donna, and Rick talking. The conversation was calm, and I heard Mack say in a serious tone, "Rick, Jesus can help you—give it all to Him, Brother."

I approached the doorway and stood, staring in silence. Finally, I asked, "Where are the boys and my parents?"

"They're gone," Rick replied. "Your mom packed the boys' things, and—hmm—they decided to head home tonight instead of tomorrow."

The boys had planned to go home with Mom and Dad anyway, but I wished they hadn't left so hastily. I was still upset with Rick and had *no* desire to stay at home that night.

Sensing my apprehension, Mack and Donna remained several hours talking things out with us. After a prayer, we walked outside together, thanking them for their support.

As their taillights disappeared into the darkness, Rick and I stood in silence. The rain had stopped, and, thankfully, the buzz from the alcohol was gone. We both felt deflated.

With a deep sigh, Rick turned to me. "Cindy, I'm sorry. I didn't mean for everything to get out of hand. I actually wanted to make everything special. The grill and smoker were fired up, the boys were having a ball, your parents were here, *and* it was really nice to see the smile on your face. But it all just snuck up on me with one piña colada here and a peach daiquiri there. You name it; I mixed it. It was supposed to be fun, but I knew better. You don't mix hard liquor like that and expect a soft landing."

Pray Big

A feeling of empty sadness washed over me as I looked up at the big sky and brilliant stars. Here I stood beside the man I'd loved and married—a man who'd confided in me on our first date how he secretly wished on every shooting star that he could somehow give his whole heart to God. But he didn't know how.

I knew Rick's apology was sincere. I *knew* the depth of his character when substance abuse didn't distort and destroy; I knew his kindness, his business acumen, and what an incredible father he was.

But he was truly trapped, and I didn't know how to help him—or to halt this cycle we kept repeating.

For the moment, though, I'd still be keeping my early morning prayer time with God—trusting Him to fulfill His promise through this setback somehow.

> Trust in the LORD with all your heart,
> And lean not on your own understanding;
> In all your ways acknowledge Him,
> And He shall direct your paths (Proverbs 3:5, 6).

Chapter 17

With summer fading and the new school year starting, I noticed Rick making changes for the better—little steps for sure, but I thanked God for each one.

For years, Rick's typical pattern included drinking beer before noon, which lasted well into the evening. He worked hard for his buzz and wanted to keep it as long as possible. To achieve this, he waited to eat until his bedtime—long after the boys were asleep.

Interestingly, several weeks after the Fourth of July setback, Rick casually asked me to start buying a variety of nonalcoholic beverages for him to drink.

Hmm, is this his way of telling me he plans to start his day with something else instead of beer? Maybe the various beverages would provide an alternative to alcohol and lessen his consumption of beer, I reasoned.

On another occasion, he suggested a meal change regarding the shared cooking duties between us as we juggled our busy family schedule. "You know, Cindy, maybe we could come up with some ideas for healthier meal options together. I'm not talking anything drastic—just something new—like a meal plan that we all can look forward to for family meals."

Again, I pondered his random requests. *If he looks forward to something new each day, maybe he will stop drinking earlier and enjoy a family meal together.*

In addition to these changes, he started coming to bed at a normal time rather than staying out all hours of the night.

Since we didn't subscribe to network programming, we watched a lot of movies—especially Westerns. Many nights, Rick crawled into bed and inserted his favorite, *Pale Rider*. Without fail, he'd fall asleep well before the final scene—unintentionally using it for sleeping medicine. Repeatedly watching the same movie bored me, but I happily endured. Having him home was a pleasant trade-off in contrast to his normal late-night back-road excursions with his buddies.

These seemingly hopeful milestones toward restoration filled my heart with thankfulness.

Still, our marriage flailed along—swinging between good and bad days. There were notable improvements but no sense of closeness or the family life I longed for. Overall, we seemed happiest doing our own thing—like ships passing in the night.

Unsurprisingly, our intimate life remained nonexistent. While I longed for physical connection with my husband, lurking thoughts of Rick's suspected pornography addiction often stabbed me with feelings of personal rejection. My heart ached for a resurrection of his fond affections.

Although my journey of forgiveness took away the buildup of anxiety in my heart, I wasn't immune to these fresh attacks. Rick's ongoing lustful cravings and his absences from home on occasion had the unnerving ability to churn up a sour taste in my mouth.

I detested his drinking, smoking, and occasional recreational drugs, but the suspected porn use wounded me particularly deep. My heart continued to cry out, *There's got to be more to life than this!*

The Iceback Sno-Shack season ended, and after a good cleaning and winterizing, we placed the trailer in storage until spring. Overall, I loved the experience, but juggling the side business with everything else in our life fatigued me. Available evenings and weekends were few and far between, and I yearned for a free Saturday to relax at home with my family.

Finally, I got my wish. But the moment my feet hit the floor that Saturday morning, it felt like an uphill battle. A never-ending flow of company filtered in and out from morning to afternoon. Despite the distractions, I continued with meal preparations.

Thinking I'd *finally* seen the last car leave, I set the table and began taking food out of the oven. *Now, maybe we can enjoy some family time together.* Excitedly, I opened the door to call the boys inside.

Surprisingly, I came face-to-face with Rick and his sidekick, Robbie. I felt my stomach knot up a little. This didn't bode well.

"Oh, hey, Robbie, I didn't know you were here," I said as I poked my head past him and out the door, trying to see the kids. "Excuse me, Robbie. Boys, the food is ready, come eat!"

Rick stepped into the house, and a strange look crossed his face as he took in the family meal setup.

"Robbie and I are going to the store to get cigarettes really quick," he announced. "We'll be back in about thirty minutes."

"Uh, well, I was just getting ready for us to sit down and eat together." I knew my disappointment showed.

"We won't be long," he said—and with that, they were gone.

So much for a family meal together.

"Boys, hurry up, come on in—the food's getting cold!"

Mealtime came and went without Rick. After eating, the boys resumed playing outside until dark. After coaxing them in for baths, we cuddled up and watched a movie together.

Hours later, the boys and I were fast asleep when a noise startled me awake at 3:00 A.M. I groggily realized the commotion and voices were Rick and Robbie in the kitchen.

Twelve hours had passed, and now the big boys were home from their thirty-minute cigarette shopping trip. Clearly, they were both drunk and ready to scuffle with each other over who knows what. It was always like this with the two of them after a day of drinking. I jumped out of bed and quickly got dressed as their voices continued to escalate.

My former inclination would've been to give Rick and Robbie a piece of my mind. Their *asinine*, idiotic behavior was *infuriating*. For a split second, my old repertoire of sarcastic phrases and caustic, judgmental words bubbled to the surface, ready to fire off my tongue.

But as I walked down the hall and through the dining room, a completely surprising thought formed, powerfully eclipsing my irritation. *I should offer to cook something for them. They're probably hungry.*

I walked into the kitchen, seeing my husband with a genuine heart I knew had come only from the Holy Spirit, and asked, "Would you like something to eat?"

Wait, did I really just say that?

Rick and Robbie stared at me and then at each other. I repeated, "Are you hungry?"

They both shrugged their shoulders and simultaneously said, "Sure!"

For the life of me, I don't remember what I cooked. But what I do remember most is not being mad, instead actually feeling compassion for them.

They had no idea what they were missing, living apart from Jesus. They didn't know life offered so much more. I wanted them to have a new life, one that offered real contentment and satisfaction.

After putting food on their plates, and a thank you from them, I returned to bed. As I drifted off to sleep, I thought about how Rick truly wanted to change but just didn't know how to make it last. It seemed as if the continual temptations and pressures were just too much for him.

The next morning, Rick woke up earlier than usual. He walked into the kitchen and gave me a perplexed look as I prepared my church potluck dish.

Crossing over to the dining-room window, he gazed out front. With his head down, he slowly turned toward me, putting both hands in his front pockets.

Before he even spoke, I knew the atmosphere was about to change. With no idea what was coming next, I swallowed hard and gave him my full attention.

"Why were you so kind to me last night?" he quietly asked.

Processing his question *and* the odd but kind look in his eyes, I replied with a deep breath, "It wasn't me being nice to you, Rick, it was Jesus. I've been spending a lot of time with Him, so thank Him."

"I can tell," he said as his eyes softened even more. "You've been different lately—and I like it—a lot."

Oh Lord, is Rick's heart finally changing? I don't want to get my hopes up, I've been let down so many times before.

I sat in church that Sunday morning, knowing that Jesus faithfully answered the cry of my heart—but not *at all* as I had planned.

When I first began fasting, I fully expected an instant transformation in my husband. Instead, God transformed *me*. He gave me a new heart—a new heart for Him and a new heart for my husband.

While I prayed for miraculous changes in my husband, God worked a miracle of change in *me*. I marched on in faith, fully expecting more blessings. Surely God *could* save to the uttermost!

In my journal, I wrote a paraphrased prayer from Psalms 103:2–5 and 19:14:

God Can Do So Much More

Bless the Lord, O my soul, and forget not all His benefits:

Who forgives all Cindy's and Rick's iniquities; who heals all Cindy's and Rick's diseases; who redeems Cindy's and Rick's life from destruction; who crowns Cindy and Rick with lovingkindness and tender mercies; who satisfies Cindy's and Rick's mouths with good things; so that Cindy's and Rick's youth is renewed like the eagle's.

Let the words of my mouth and the meditation of my heart be acceptable in Your sight, O God, my Strength and my Redeemer. In Jesus' name, amen.

Dave checked in with me often, assuring me he *and* others were praying for my family. One day, I took a leap of faith and confided in him about the precious impression God gave me at the Christmas party.

"Dave, *you* might be the one to reach my husband! Something *is* changing with Rick—I can see it!"

Little did I know the Holy Spirit was up to *something more* than I could ever think or imagine! And Dave would *indeed* play a huge role.

Chapter 18

With a long Monday at work nearly over, I finished up some last-minute restocking duties in the operating room. Most everyone had left for the day, and the peace and quiet provided concentrated time for prayer while I worked.

Suddenly, the hallway phone began to ring.

Grrr, I hope that isn't a doctor or the anesthesia group calling to add on a surgery right now. It was my turn for late-day rotation, meaning I was on duty in case of a patient emergency.

I picked up the phone cautiously. *Please don't let it be a doctor, please, please, please!*

"Ambulatory Surgery Center, this is Cindy."

"Hey, Cindy, this is Dave," he said with his usual upbeat cheerfulness. "I'm so glad you answered!"

"Hey, Dave, what's up?" *Bummer, it is an add-on*, I thought.

"Is Rick at the house right now?" Dave asked.

Shock wiped my mind clean. "What? I mean, I don't know—I haven't talked to him today. We've been really busy over here," I said.

"OK, well, I'm going to run down to your house and see if I can catch him at home," he responded.

"Oh!" I said, trying to process my reeling thoughts. "Wow, OK, great! Uh, Dave, I know you've seen our house on your way to Monticello, but you do know it's a sixty-mile round trip, right? I just wouldn't want you to waste your time," I said.

"Hey, no worries—really! I'm praying I'll find him there! Talk to you later!" His enthusiasm was evident.

I slowly placed the phone back on the receiver, lost in thought. *What was all that about? You're praying you'll find him home, Dave? I'm praying you'll find him there! Are you kidding me? Thank You, Jesus!*

My whole face felt like one big smile as I floated to the break room to grab a leftover bagel. I plopped down on the comfy couch and commenced one of the most urgent prayers of my life.

Dear Lord, please *let Rick be home, amen.*

About an hour later, I left work and drove over to Lowe's home-improvement store to pick up a few fall mums. As I exited my car, I looked up and saw *Dave* walking out of the store!

Immediately my heart sank. *Oh no! Rick must not have been home, or maybe Dave didn't go at all!*

"Hey, Cindy! I didn't expect to see you here," he greeted me.

"Uh, yeah, me either, I mean, I didn't expect to see you here either. Did you go see Rick?" I asked.

The smile on his face grew even bigger. "Yes! Rick was home, and we had a great visit!"

Amazing, God! This guy works fast! He drove sixty miles, visited with my husband, finished his shopping, and here we are in the parking lot talking about it!

Dave was still speaking. "As a matter of fact, I told Rick he'd been on my heart, and I wondered if he'd be willing to give me one hour a week to study the Bible together."

My brain struggled to keep up—I simply couldn't believe what I was hearing!

Afraid of the answer, I fumbled out, "What did he say, Dave?"

His face glowed. "He said yes!"

I felt like I was free-falling into joy. "Rick said yes! Really?"

In that instant, I knew that once again, my life had changed forever. I felt the awesome awareness of God personally answering my heart's deepest longing. The ordinary surroundings of Lowe's parking lot felt like sacred ground as I caught this glimpse of Him working through my prayers.

Dave and I visited a few moments longer, and I told him I'd be in touch soon. Joyfully, I picked up my mums and headed home. On the drive home, I debated what I should say to Rick when I got home.

Pray Big

Hey honey, how was your visit with Dave? Too abrupt.

How was your day? Did anything exciting happen? How lame.

I'm so excited you said yes to studying the Bible with Dave! Umm, no.

Nothing seemed appropriate. Even worse, doubts crept in, and I worried Rick would change his mind—or confess he said yes just to get rid of Dave. As I prayed, I half-heartedly prepared for the many excuses Rick would probably offer.

Yet, despite these shreds of doubt, I couldn't shake the impression that maybe this was the beginning of "something more"—just as I'd been praying all this time. I buzzed around the curve near our house, and my heart felt light.

The boys were playing outside, and Rick was down at the chicken houses. *Boy, am I nervous! Please, Lord, let everything go well with our conversation about Dave.*

After a little more playtime, I called the boys inside so Tyler could start his homework while I prepared dinner. Rick came in and out several times to grab a beer and make small talk. But whenever I tried to bring up the subject of Bible studies, my lips froze.

Dinnertime was unusually quiet that night other than the boys bantering back and forth about their day. Rick still had chores to finish, so I retreated to the recliner to unwind.

Soon enough, it was time to scoot the boys through their baths and bedtime prayers. After waiting all evening for the right moment to talk to Rick about Dave, I concluded the timing was off and decided to wait until the next day.

I finished my nighttime routine and entered our bedroom, finding Rick already in bed with the light off.

Quietly pulling back the comforter, I slipped under the sheets and pulled the covers up to my neck. Looking up toward the ceiling, I let out a sigh into the dark. *I wonder why he hasn't said anything about Dave's visit. Should I bring it up now?*

Without even realizing I was going to speak, I suddenly heard words flowing out of my mouth. "I know Dave stopped by today—so—when are we going to start Bible studies?"

Silence.

I held my breath as I waited—the moment stretched almost unbearably.

Then Rick spoke. "Why don't we start this Thursday night?"

What? O, Lord! Yes! Yes! Silently, but with a smile beaming across my face in the darkness, I gave another figurative high five to God. I tried to speak casually.

"OK, great! I'll let him know—hopefully, tomorrow. Good night."

"Good night," Rick echoed back.

Everything in me wanted to jump up and down on the bed like a little kid, belting out the "Hallelujah" chorus at the top of my lungs! I refrained.

But a full orchestra of praise built to crescendo in my heart. Joy overflowed as I anticipated the days ahead, *I can't wait to see Dave tomorrow! He's going to be thrilled!*

Sure enough, as I entered the break room the next morning, there was Dave—alone.

"Hey, Dave! Guess what? Rick wants to start studying the Bible *this week*! Can you come Thursday night?"

"Cindy! That's great news! Yes—yes! Name the time, and I'll be there!" His excitement matched mine.

I had known Dave was different for a long time now, but watching his face at that moment, I understood even more deeply how special his love for God and others made him.

We agreed upon a time and, just like that, Rick and Cindy Mercer were all set for their first Bible study *ever* as husband and wife.

Chapter 19

In the days that followed, an unspoken sense of anxiousness and excitement mingled in my heart. *I hope Rick isn't getting cold feet and wanting to back out of our commitment. God, please be our constant help—protect this appointment.*

Thursday arrived. I came home from work, and my gaze automatically flew to the beer carton in the entryway, noticing only nine or ten beers, at most, gone. For years, I'd glanced at it when I came home because it helped me to gauge what type of mood I might expect from Rick throughout the evening.

I sure hope he doesn't act up or say anything inappropriate to Dave. I really wish he could just not *drink for one day! Please, Lord, let everything go well tonight.*

After spending time with the boys, I tidied up the house, made a quick dinner, and went to talk with God. It felt like my whole life hinged on this monumental evening. I knelt by my bed and poured my heart out.

When I arose, I felt both peace and a great expectation. I walked toward the kitchen with high hopes.

Dave arrived right on time that crisp November evening with his Bible in hand. Making small talk, Rick and I invited him in and led the way to our dining-room table.

Again, I worried about Rick's drinking and what Dave must be thinking.

Surely, he smelled the alcohol. As Dave walked past me, he gave me a reassuring glance as if to say, "I'm aware, but it's OK, don't worry."

Rick sat at the head of the table with Dave to his right. I sat down across from Dave. Silence fell momentarily. *This is awkward, God. What are we doing? Please help us. We need it so bad.*

Sensing the discomfort building between Rick and me, Dave asked in his easygoing way if he could start our study with a prayer.

As soon as he finished, the built-up tension disintegrated. I thanked God for this small miracle of encouragement as we began.

Dave opened his Bible and handed us each a lesson guide from *In His Word* titled "Is There Anything We Can Trust?" I felt drawn to the attractive illustration of an open Bible with the world positioned above it surrounded by blue sky and stars.[1]

We began reading together, and soon, the powerful message drew all three of us into lively conversation. I jotted down notes and underlined phrases:

- *Someone recently observed that everything once fastened down has come loose.*
- *There doesn't seem to be anyone or anything you can trust.*
- *There is something you can believe in, and there is someone you can trust.*
- *There is a book in the world that you can trust: that Book is the Bible.*
- *The Bible is God's message of love and truth to His earthbound children. This is His way of making known to us what His plan and will are for our lives.*
- *You can trust the Bible.*

"Man shall not live by bread alone, but by every word that proceeds from the mouth of God" (Matthew 4:4).

"And you shall know the truth, and the truth shall make you free" (John 8:32).

    It is only as the Spirit leads us in the study of the Bible, interpreting to us what He inspired the writers to put down for us, that we will know the truth of God's plan for our lives.

Throughout the lesson, additional phrases and scriptures leaped off the pages into my heart. *Lord, I hope the same thing is happening to Rick right now!*

The study made it clear that God's promises would help us fight our battles. I felt especially encouraged when we discovered the Holy Spirit would guide us into *all* truth (John 16:13).

Oh, how we need that!

We also read how God's Word offers assurance in helping us understand the Scriptures *and* His plan for our lives. Our study concluded with two verses:

> Your word I have hidden in my heart,
> That I might not sin against You . . .
> Your word is a lamp to my feet,
> And a light to my path" (Psalm 119:11, 105).

Dave kept his one-hour commitment and concluded with prayer. As he stood up, he handed us our next lesson so we could study in the days ahead—"Is There Anyone We Can Trust?"[2] We thanked him for coming and ended our evening on a refreshingly positive note.

After some cuddle time with the boys, Rick and I went to the bedroom at the same time and lightly discussed a few lesson highlights from the night.

I drifted off to sleep in a warm, comforting glow. Hope was surely on the horizon.

Each lesson guide included a series of questions with corresponding Bible verses and a place to write down the answers. Each day, I completed a few questions during my study time and very much enjoyed the process.

I didn't know what Rick was doing with his guide and felt too hesitant to ask. I didn't want to risk rocking the boat and having him back out.

The week passed quickly. Soon the night of our second appointment arrived, bringing Dave and his Bible to our dining-room table again.

Although Rick hadn't filled in his lesson at all (no surprise), he listened with focused attention. He also joined in the discussion regularly as we covered verses characterizing God:

- 2 Chronicles 2:5, 6—*God is great.*
- Mark 10:27—*All things are possible with God.*
- Psalm 147:3–5—*He heals the brokenhearted and calls the stars by name. His understanding is infinite.*
- Malachi 3:6—*He does not change.*

- James 1:17—*All good gifts are from Him; there is no variableness with Him.*

A comment in the lesson touched my heart. "With a God like this in control of the world, what have we to fear?"[3]

"If God is for us, who can be against us?" (Romans 8:31).

Before he left, Dave again handed us our next lesson guide, titled "How in the World Did We Get Into This Mess?"[4] I diligently studied my lesson and filled in my answers.

When Dave arrived the next week for our third evening together, I felt a surprising burst of happiness when Rick pulled out *his* lesson guide as well. He'd apparently *also* studied and filled in some answers.

The final question on the back page was: "What three things do you most look forward to about being in the new earth?"[5]

Rick wrote his answer in two columns, side by side. In the first, he wrote, "Love, Joy, Peace"; and in the second, "Father, Son, Holy Ghost."

At the very bottom of the page, the lesson concluded with a commitment statement: "I want to be an 'heir' and receive the promise of being part of God's everlasting kingdom."

My heart overflowed as I read my husband's simple one-word answer: "Yes."

In the space to fill in your name and address, he wrote, "Rick Mercer, Sinful Earth."

This night marked a profound turning point in both our study and our marriage. We no longer did the lessons separately. Instead, we began reading through the questions and answers together.

After putting the boys to bed, we'd head to the bedroom and start our new lesson for the next week. When the question referenced Romans 8:38, we read verse 38, plus all of chapter 8. Sometimes, we even covered Romans 7 and 9 to gain a clearer picture of the study topic.

Then we'd discuss what we were learning. *Never* in the history of our marriage had we talked together this deeply or enjoyed such rewarding conversations. It was both fascinating and illuminating to see this new side of my husband as he processed through the truths we were studying.

The atmosphere in our home changed dramatically as we progressed week by week. For so long, Satan imprisoned us in fear and pain—each isolated in our miserable loneliness.

Now we both felt God becoming Commander in Charge of our home and hearts. Together, each in different ways, we gained new spiritual heights—and it felt wonderful.

Driving home from work one evening, I marveled at the amazing change in my life from those darkest days in the pit of despair. I reviewed the journey of healing and restoration—and I rejoiced in awe.

Gone was my bitterness, hurt, and anger. Gone was my hesitancy to trust God with every gritty detail of my insecurities, pain, and resentment. The magnitude of difference astounded me.

Thank You, God, for what You are doing in my life, Rick's life, and our life together. In Jesus' name, amen.

By now, neither of us could deny the extreme differences occurring. We knew the source for our newfound joy was our life in Jesus, His Word, and the Holy Spirit.

> "Behold, I will do a new thing,
> Now it shall spring forth;
> Shall you not know it?
> I will even make a road in the wilderness
> And rivers in the desert" (Isaiah 43:19).

This flowing, living water entered the dry recesses of Rick's heart and awakened his thirst for more. Onward we studied—about love and law, grace and redemption, how sin imprisoned us and how only God could set us free.

Rick understood how it felt to be chained by the habits and desires he hated. Paul's words in Romans about deliverance from the power of sinful nature through the death of Jesus particularly touched his heart.

When we studied about being born again, he wrote, "New! The old you is dead! All is new!" And in the margin, "Victory through Christ!"

At the bottom of that lesson, he added, "The weight of the past is heavy and can ruin you, even to death. Through Jesus, this burden can be lifted, and this day can be the first day of the rest of your life for eternity!"

God Can Do So Much More

By lesson 17, our hearts—and address—were changed forever: *"Rick and Cindy Mercer, Sinful Earth Forward to New Jerusalem!"*

1. "Is There Anything We Can Trust?" *In His Word*, Seminars Unlimited.
2. "Is There Anyone We Can Trust?" *In His Word*, Seminars Unlimited.
3. "Is There Anyone We Can Trust?"
4. "How in the World Did We Get Into This Mess?" *In His Word*, Seminars Unlimited.
5. "How in the World Did We Get Into This Mess?"

Chapter 20

The 2003 holiday season arrived with a wonderful presence in the air of hope and restoration! My heart rejoiced at the marked improvements at home. The time flew by, and because of our focused Bible-study time with Dave, I almost forgot about the annual Christmas party!

Planning began later than usual, but I jumped in anyway at the last minute to help. But a big problem arose—my heart was far from party preparation. I really had no desire to go.

I cringed every time friends at work asked, "Rick's going to be our bartender again this year, right?" That was the last thing he needed to do!

Even though we'd only been studying with Dave for a short period of time, it just didn't seem right to go. God was speaking to Rick's heart and moving in powerful ways, despite his continued use of nicotine and alcohol. He still drank every day, but the quantity and frequency declined. Going to the party wouldn't change that, but it felt almost hypocritical.

We could just go to the party for dinner like Dave and Lisa did last year! Yes! That's what we could do. Deep down, it was a great thought, but I knew that if we went, wild horses wouldn't keep my husband away from the bar.

A million explanations ran through my mind to politely excuse us from the party. However, none of them seemed right. *Lord, You know I don't want to go to the party this year, and I'm ashamed of being a coward and not just saying no to everyone. Please provide a way of escape so we don't have to go. In Jesus' name, amen.*

God Can Do So Much More

During the day on Friday, while I was at work, Rick drank his normal quota of beer. By the time I arrived home, *he* seemed eager to wrap up his chores and get the show on the road. But, I kept praying for an outlet to exempt us from the party, just hoping for a miracle.

But, by 5:00 P.M., it was time for us to get dressed up for the party and head to town. Every step I took that day felt heavy. *Lord! I don't want to go!*

Rick was still finishing up in the bathroom, so I waited on him in the kitchen with a "not so excited" attitude.

"Well, I guess I'm ready, let's go," Rick said as I whirled around to look at him. He looked really nice all dressed up, but a concerning glance on his face troubled me.

"What's wrong? You don't look so good." I said with concern.

All of a sudden, he darted around the corner to the boys' bathroom and began to vomit. *Uh oh, this isn't good.* I rushed to the door, surveying the episode, and said, "Honey, are you OK?"

He barely managed to mumble, "I don't think I'm going anywhere tonight. I feel awful!" As I opened the bathroom cabinet, grabbed a washcloth, and began to hold it under the running water, I realized *We're not going to the party! Oh, wait—I feel bad, I didn't want him to get sick, Lord, just some other simple excuse would've worked!*

Nevertheless, a phone call to a coworker excused us for the evening. Rick decided to lay down on the couch, and I changed into my comfy pj's and joined him in the living room. I was sprawled out in the recliner, dozing partially while watching a movie when something significant Rick said as we left last year's party popped into my mind.

"Who knows, I might not even be drinking this time next year." I sat straight up in the chair and looked over at Rick sleeping. Well, it was "next year," *and* technically speaking, he wasn't drinking at that moment. Under the original circumstances, had we gone to the party, he would be "loose as a goose."

However, something very different was transpiring in our lives—we were studying the Bible, and our home environment was *noticeably* different.

After a short break during Christmas and New Year's, we resumed our Bible studies with expectations of an exciting 2004.

Rick continued to welcome spiritual conversations into his life and initiated discussions regarding various Bible topics. Our marriage was on a positive upswing, and with each passing day, bright spots appeared. He even started attending church more.

Since I taught Sunday School at the Methodist church, I had to arrive early. But I was elated when he slipped in the backdoor just in time for the service. As he put his arm around me and sat with the boys and his parents, I couldn't help but silently say, *Thank You, Lord, I've been waiting a long time for this!*

Rick eventually became more and more comfortable with Dave's friendship and suggested we invite him; his wife, Lisa; and his boys Jake and Jordan, over for dinner. I was excited and very nervous. I knew Dave and his family were vegetarians, so I had no idea what to prepare—except for a salad. After expressing my concerns about menu options, my husband said "not to worry," and that he'd "take care of it." He was a good cook and loved doing it.

We agreed to work together so Dave's family could have a wonderful meal in harmony with their diet regimen. As the anticipated evening arrived, Rick and I worked side by side in the kitchen. I made a big, colorful salad, some rice, and a dessert, while Rick was in charge of making his wonderful Crock-Pot pinto beans.

After my contributions were complete, I cheerfully set the table with some brand-new dishes I'd bought specifically for the occasion. The yellow salad plates coordinated beautifully with the gorgeous dinner plates imprinted with deep, rich-colored fruit. *Perfect! They'll never know I just bought them.* I wanted something better for our company than my old array of hodgepodge dishes.

"Honey, are the beans done? I see Dave and his family pulling in the driveway now," I said with a trace of stress!

Oh, boy, I'm so nervous! What if they don't like our food?

"Yep, everything is good here. Can you get me an extra plate?" he asked.

There was a knock at the door. "Here." I passed him a plate as I walked to answer the door. "What do you want that for?" I asked.

I almost gasped when I looked over and saw Rick pulling the ham hock out of the beans and placing it on the plate only moments before our company walked in.

He looked at me with a smile and said, "They're vegetarians, you know."

The evening couldn't have gone better! Dave even asked for an extra helping of the "tasty beans"! The boys played well together, and we talked for what seemed like hours.

As they left that night, they kindly thanked us for the hospitality *and* the delicious meal!

We followed them outside to their car, hoping there would be more dinners together. *What a nice Christian family*, I thought as they left to go home.

God Can Do So Much More

The weeks rolled on together, and we learned life-changing truths and built new foundations for our marriage. Individually, my private prayer and study life developed, and I continued fasting when prompted by the Holy Spirit. As I delighted myself in the Lord, He faithfully gave me the desires of my heart (Psalm 37:4).

Over time, Dave asked if he could bring Gary and Dr. Samuel along for our Bible-study time. He informed us that we would be studying some in-depth topics, and he thought they would offer valuable insights into the upcoming lessons. Rick didn't know them, but since I worked with them the same length of time as Dave, I assured my husband he would like them too.

On the nights they came with Dave, their input invited well-rounded discussions, wisdom, and rich application for our study. We grew to love and covet our Thursday-night appointments around our dining room table.

One of Rick's growing concerns was a possible condemnation of his lifestyle choices from Dave, Gary, and Dr. Samuel. He was still drinking and was under the enemy's ensnarement of lust. However, his mannerisms and sleeping habits *indicated* drugs were on the decline, if not gone completely. However, he was smart enough to know that they probably had his number on a few things. He had started slacking off his drinking on Thursdays a little earlier than normal. But he waited—almost expecting them to chastise or at least call him out on a few things.

But—they never did. Not even once. Instead, they continually and faithfully pointed my husband to Jesus. They allowed the Holy Spirit to do the convicting work in Rick's heart, always reminding him, "It's all about Jesus!" And telling him, "Jesus loves you, Rick!"

Chapter 21

Watching Rick discover precious Bible gems fascinated me. His hunger for more was contagious! However, the sins separating him from Jesus consumed his thoughts almost daily. As I observed these struggles from a distance, I wanted to help him—but I couldn't. He had his own battles to fight, so I chose to "assist" him through intercessory prayer.

Even though we prayed at meals and every Bible study, I overheard Rick say to Dave, "I'm not praying for myself. I'm not sure how to do that." These comments assured me he *wanted* his own personal prayer life.

In addition, we weren't praying together as a couple. In the beginning, we'd prayed on our first date and a few other times effortlessly, but now with the passing of so much time and many hurdles, the simple act terrified me.

The very thought of talking out loud to God with my husband felt daunting for some reason—actually awkward. Considering my individual relationship with Jesus, I knew it wasn't normal to feel this way. *I know we* should *be praying together, Lord, so why the reluctance?*

Neither of us discussed the concern, but an unspoken urgency in our hearts to connect with God on a new level prevailed.

One evening we were in bed, reviewing an upcoming lesson, when a period of unusual silence filled the room. With sweaty palms and a lump in my throat, I gave myself a pep talk. *Just do it, Cindy. Go ahead—ask Rick to pray! What are you waiting on?*

Lord, I don't know what to do, this feels so strange. Why am I so nervous?

God Can Do So Much More

We exchanged glances, and within seconds, we reached for each other's hands. We both knew what was coming. After a few seconds, we slipped out of bed and made the awkward transition to our knees. For a moment, it felt like a first date—and, in many ways, it was!

Unsure of the whole process, I bravely prayed with an audible, trembling voice. With our hands still clasped together, I tightened my grip. "Dear Lord, I want to thank You and praise You for blessing me with Rick and for Your outpouring of mercy and grace. Please help us to be faithful in the days ahead. In Jesus' name, amen."

Whew! That wasn't so bad.

My brief prayer was followed by a few seconds of silence.

Now, Rick's quivering voice articulated his prayer for me, "Dear Lord, I can never thank You enough for my precious wife. I'm so thankful for her many prayers. I want to be the man You designed me to be—and the husband she deserves. Thank You for hearing our prayers, in Jesus' name, amen."

I've waited years for this moment—I don't want this to end!

I thought for sure I'd crumble in his arms as I heard him pray.

After the "amen," we lingered in a tight embrace, recognizing a seismic shift had taken place. Although uncomfortable at first, this interaction transformed into a flourishing new foundation for our marriage.

Satan had a plan. And it didn't include us praying together. His "hostage" situation over our prayer life started dissolving right before our very eyes. Yes, it was uncomfortable, but it was so worth it!

The enemy tried everything possible to keep us from filling the golden bowl in heaven with the incense of our prayers. His desired destruction of our marriage was at the top of his list. And he almost succeeded. But God said, "No, you can't have Rick and Cindy; they belong to Me!"

Rick and I agreed to pray and study together daily, knowing it would help us weather future storms. Over time, the bondage was completely broken, and there was no room for the enemy anymore. All praise, thanksgiving, and glory were given to God!

We gave God full permission to do what He always wanted to do—kick Satan out of our marriage.

My heart could barely contain composure when Rick started telling me, "God is doing something in my heart I've never experienced before. I want to give Him my all!"

As powerful Bible truths saturated our lives, God's light shined brightly in our darkness. A new day dawned as we embarked on a beautiful new journey together!

Chapter 22

headed for the medicine room after my last surgery case when I heard someone holler my name.

"Cindy—call for you on the hallway phone!"

"Hello, this is Cindy. Oh hey, honey, what's up?" I asked.

"Are you busy?" Rick inquired.

"Nope, not at all, just finished up lunch," I replied.

"OK, great" There was a deep breath from Rick. "Cindy, you aren't going to believe what just happened," he said seriously.

"Well, I'm waiting. What is it?" I anxiously questioned.

"I'm having a bonfire," he said with great enthusiasm!

What is he up to? What's the big deal about having a bonfire? I silently wondered.

"Great! The boys will be excited when they get off the school bus," I said.

"Hmm, probably not. The fire will be long gone by the time they arrive home. . . Cindy, I just declared war on something that's had a grip on my life for a very long time—since I was a teenager. For years, I've had a big collection of movies and magazines that controlled my life. None of it is good. My entire attitude toward our relationship has been warped and manipulated by this distraction from the enemy. But it's gone—all of it, for good! And—you won't believe the horrible stench that is coming from the burning pile right now. I'm watching it all become part of my past forever," he said.

My heart beat faster as I prayed. *This is incredible, Lord! What do I say? This certainly answers a lot of questions for me. But how do I respond to a confession like this?*

"Are you serious? This is amazing! I'm *really* proud of you and have been praying for you for a long time! I can't wait to give you a hug; I'll hurry home as soon as I can!" I exclaimed.

Well, I sure wasn't expecting that kind of a phone call. Thank You, Jesus, for Your overcoming power!

Years of suspicions accompanied by feelings of rejection were all confirmed in one phone call. For too long, the enemy robbed my husband of a healthy attitude toward intimacy, convincing him to cave in to the pressure. The forbidden, secret sin was exposed, and we were experiencing another great leap toward victory. God was truly providing a pathway of hope and restoration.

This is some of the best news ever. I'm not sure what happens next, but I'm ready! Thank You, Lord, for this breakthrough. Keep surprising me with Your love!

My thoughts traveled a million miles away as I walked down the operating room hall. Reflections of God's ability to resurrect hope captivated me: finding the love of my life; restoration of our family; God speaking when I couldn't take anymore; my internal heart change; the healing power of forgiveness; Dave's prayers; Rick saying yes to Bible studies; our decision to pray together; and now this—freedom from drugs and pornography!

But still, I knew God had something more.

Springtime in the South arrived, bringing baseball season back in full view. My excitement level was over the top because I'd partnered with local ballfield officials to sell shaved ice on Saturdays. This was particularly profitable but time-consuming.

The big day in April finally arrived to make my debut with the Iceback Sno-Shack at the ball complex. Rick went with me early to set everything up, and once the water and electricity hookups were in working order, he returned home.

Perfect, bring on the customers; this is going to be a great day!

Several hours and a steady stream of customers later, I was surprised to see Rick walking toward me wearing khakis and a polo shirt.

Why is he here so soon? It's hours from closing time. And why is he wearing those clothes? That's really strange.

No one was waiting in line for shaved ice, so I stepped outside to see what he was up to.

"Hey, whatcha doing here so early, and what's with the clothes? This is a ball field, you know," I said with a grin.

With a huge smile, he replied, "I'm going to church in Pine Bluff, where Dave, Gary, and Dr. Samuel go."

"Seriously? But they haven't invited us to church yet," I said.

"We don't have to be invited to go to church," he said with a chuckle.

"Wait, you're going to church without *me*?" I asked.

Still smiling he replied, "Yep, but don't worry, I'll be back later and help you finish up," he said, as he walked back toward the truck.

I stood there in disbelief of what I was hearing and seeing!

I don't know what You're doing, Lord, but I sure like it!

As promised, several hours later, he returned with a mixture of good *and* bad news. Rick filled me in on his day while we closed up shop, "Cindy, you should've seen the look on everyone's face when I walked into church today. They were so surprised! I really enjoyed it there, and I know you and the boys will too."

"I'm looking forward to it, there aren't any ball games here next week, so we should be able to go," I said cheerfully.

"Great! Well, on a different note, I received some really bad news after leaving the church. I found out Wayne passed away this morning from an apparent heart attack."

"Oh no, that's horrible! I'm so sorry, honey, I know you've been good friends for a long time. Hey, what did Wayne say to you several months ago?" I asked.

"Hmm, yeah. I was actually thinking about that on the way home. I told him several months ago I'd started studying the Bible, and he said he could see me becoming a preacher," Rick said somberly.

"Interesting he would say something like that, don't you think?" I observed.

"I would say so—I'm going to miss him a lot. Wayne was a great friend who maybe saw something in me I couldn't possibly imagine. It's just so hard to believe he's gone," he said.

On the outside, Wayne looked like a picture of health. But at the young age of forty, he was gone—leaving a beautiful wife and two young children behind.

Ironically, we were learning biblical health principles, which we'd considered implementing, plus we were interested in a new lifestyle. With the shock of Wayne's sudden death fresh on his mind, Rick asked me to schedule him an appointment with my doctor right away.

Being one to avoid getting his blood pressure checked and doctors altogether, this was nothing short of a miracle! Rick's face maintained a dark shade of red, and he consumed large amounts of high-fat, fried foods. In addition, other concerning habits such as Rick's alcohol consumption left me worried often about his health.

At the clinic, the nurse informed him his blood pressure was high and encouraged him to modify his meal choices. On top of that, a few weeks later, to my husband's surprise but not mine, his lab results revealed a cholesterol level of 287, and his triglyceride level was 518.

"Rick, you're at high risk for a heart attack or stroke," the doctor emphasized.

The stern warning for dietary changes, plus a new prescription for Crestor, was a sobering wake-up call for my husband. Being the same age as Wayne, he took the warning seriously.

Rick took his medicine faithfully but wasn't thrilled about it. Two weeks later, he decided there must be a better way. Together, we decided to start eating healthier instead of taking medicine. Food items deemed biblically unclean were removed from our normal menu lineup, meaning no more pork, crawfish, or catfish. Also, we fully cooked our steaks instead of eating them medium-rare. A variety of vegetables were added into our nightly dinners, and within several months, we were delighted to discover marked improvements in his lab values. We had a long way to go, but purposeful efforts to change were incorporated.

The obvious outward transformations in Rick didn't go unnoticed by people in our small community. The positive comments coming from family and friends encouraged him and confirmed God was working powerfully in our lives.

Praises flowed freely to God for the many milestones and transformational changes witnessed. My husband was becoming a brand-new man!

Even though incremental dietary changes occurred, alcohol, cigarettes, and smokeless tobacco lingered in his life.

Although he drank and smoked less, I desperately wanted him to have total victory.

Knowing Jesus provided a way for everyone to overcome, I reasoned He'd surely make a way for Rick. Realizing how close he was to tasting freedom, I enthusiastically claimed Philippians 4:13 over my husband's life, *Rick can do all things through Christ who strengthens him.*

I could see the "want to" in my husband's eyes, but the alcohol held an especially tight grip. Nothing I could do or say would make him stop—that approach hadn't worked.

Thankfully, my faith in Rick's victory wasn't in my husband—my faith was in Jesus. I trusted God to rescue him from the remaining addictions.

Armed with prayer and God's Word, I watched and waited for God's promise to be fulfilled.

Chapter 23

Before we knew it, work, home, and church commitments mounted. I was still involved with Wednesday-night Kids Church, Sunday-night Bible study, and teaching obligations at the Methodist church in addition to countless other responsibilities.

We desperately needed a reprieve from the hectic pace. To my delight, I discovered the remedy as I settled into the pew on my first Saturday morning visit to the Pine Bluff Seventh-day Adventist Church.

The attractive bulletin insert advertising an upcoming church-district campout on Lake Ouachita intrigued me. The boys took the paper from my hands and mulled it over too.

"This looks really fun!" I exclaimed.

We stood for the opening song, and my mind trailed off with hopeful thoughts. *This would be perfect for our family! Hopefully, we can go!*

After a welcoming fellowship lunch following church, Lisa and Gary's wife, Jan, filled us in on the campout details. Their enticing invitation was hard to resist.

The next day we decided to go. Excitement roared as we planned for the weekend getaway. Unfortunately, a prior commitment to help Donna with a women's event at her church the same weekend dampened my spirits briefly.

The concern was short-lived—I decided I could easily to do both!

Eager to meet new friends and escape from the fast pace, we loaded up the truck on Friday, May 7, and headed to the campout. We couldn't get there fast enough!

Pray Big

Plus, we were looking forward to meeting the pastor. Since his time was divided in a three-church district, our paths hadn't crossed. Although he was highly regarded, his absence didn't appear to leave the church in a bind. The church was blessed with active leaders who went the extra mile to welcome us, and now we were headed two hours north to spend a whole weekend with them!

The boys were bursting with excitement as we skirted around sharp curves and up and down the hills. We continued following the winding road to the campsite, enjoying the peaceful scenery of huge evergreens, mountains, lakes, and big boulders that Reece called big, fluffy rocks.

Within minutes of pulling into the day area, a man with a super-wide grin wearing a cowboy hat, boots, and shorts approached us as we came to a stop.

"Uh, hello there" he extended his hand through the passenger truck window, "I'm Pastor Ross Harris. And who might you folks be?" he inquired heartily.

We exchanged introductions and found him to be super friendly! Moments later, he accompanied us to our tent site and helped us unload our camping gear. Within a short time, others pitched in and helped too. Many new families from the other two churches in the district were present, providing lots of playmates for the boys!

Not long after settling in, the dinner bell rang. Walking over to the food tent, I spotted Jan right away. I had already heard she was a fantastic cook, and after one taste of her potato soup served up in yummy bread bowls, I knew it was true!

This campout is wonderful and just what our family needed, Lord, time with nice Christian families!

Later that night, we sat under the star-filled sky around the warm campfire singing and enjoying the company of our new friends. Pastor Terry Nelson, the guest speaker from Kalamazoo, Michigan, kicked off the weekend with an encouraging, hope-filled message.

Snuggling into our sleeping bags that Friday night, I couldn't help but wonder what was next for our family. Listening to the happy voices in nearby tents, coupled with the giggles of our boys, brought a sense of calmness over me.

Saturday morning arrived extra early for me since I needed to travel to Pine Bluff to help Donna.

Gathering a few shower items, I slipped out of the tent. I had planned to shower and ease out of the campground quietly. But as I exited the changing area, I noticed Dave's wife, Lisa, brushing her teeth.

"Hey, Cindy, everything all right," she asked?

"Oh yes, I just have to run to Pine Bluff for a few hours. Rick's sister needs my help with an event at her church. Unfortunately, it's been planned for a while. I probably should've arranged for someone to take my place. Please forgive me, I feel really bad about leaving, but I'll be back just as soon as I can," I replied.

With a genuine smile, she said, "It's OK. We'll miss you, but we understand. I was hoping you'd be here this afternoon for Jake's baptism. He's accepted Jesus into his heart and wants to give the rest of his life to Him." Beaming, she continued, "We'll be across the lake at the conference campgrounds, Camp Yorktown Bay, in case you make it back in time."

"I really apologize, I'll be praying everything goes well," I said, walking out the door. *That was super awkward. I hope I didn't hurt Lisa's feelings. I really should've made other arrangements. Baptism is a really big deal, Cindy.*

After telling Rick goodbye, I quickly left the campground—still feeling torn in two different directions. All of my reasoning to stretch myself between both events suddenly felt unwarranted. *The reason you came on the campout was to take a break, Cindy, and now look at you.* Another conundrum for sure. *There's nothing you can do about it now, just make the best of it and move on*, I resolved.

The event at Donna's church went great. Thankfully, it ended sooner than expected! *Great, I'll make it back before dark!*

Settling in behind the wheel, I made the trek back to the campout at Mountain Pine. Thoughts of Rick and the boys and Jake's baptism occupied the driving time. I focused on the joy of helping Donna, who'd been a great support and friend to me for so long, plus I knew the boys and Rick were having a fun day with great people. I looked forward to getting back and hearing all about their day!

I pulled into the campground shortly after 3:00 P.M. and was eagerly greeted by the boys and Rick as I hopped out of the truck.

"We've had so much fun!" they shrieked.

"Awesome, tell me everything! I sure missed you," I said, giving them hugs.

As they chattered away telling me their stories, I couldn't help but notice the glow on Rick's face. *I'm so glad they had fun today!* My heart was happy. But it seemed, there was something more waiting to be told. A palpable sense of elation permeated our conversation, building in intensity rapidly.

"Go ahead, Dad, tell her!" the boys chimed in unison.

"Tell me what?" I asked in return.

A huge grin formed on Rick's face, followed by a great big hug. "You're not going to believe what happened today!" he said, beaming from ear to ear.

"You should've seen all of Jake's family and friends surrounding him for his special day earlier!"

Rick could hardly contain his enthusiasm as he expressed what unfolded next.

"Right after Pastor Ross baptized Jake, Pastor Nelson stood up and made an altar call. He asked if anyone wanted a fresh, new start with Jesus. I'm not sure what happened, Cindy, but the next thing I knew, I stood up and walked down the gravel aisle toward the pastor. And there overlooking the lake, I said 'Yes, I want a fresh new start!' Then Pastor Nelson put his hands on my shoulders and said a special prayer for me."

He continued with more descriptions of the day, "After opening my eyes, I noticed three wooden crosses on an island behind us, and then I turned to face the crowd. As I looked up toward everyone looking back at me, my eyes instantly locked in on Dave's brother, Dan. He was standing at the top of the outdoor amphitheater, and all I could see were tears streaming down his face. I found out later today that he and Dave's sister Diane had people from their churches in Texas praying for me. Can you believe that?"

"Oh, honey, that is so exciting! What a special day for you—and Jake! I don't know what to say, this is amazing! Praise God for what He is doing in your life. I wish I could have seen it all!" I exclaimed.

The remainder of the day lingered with an atmosphere of unsurmountable hope!

Later that evening at dinner, we discovered that immediately before the baptism, Dave, Jake, Dan, Pastor Ross, and Pastor Nelson prayed specifically for Rick to respond and give his heart to Jesus.

Sunday morning dawned way too soon. After breakfast, we assembled around the campfire one last time for Pastor Nelson's final message.

In the midst of the crackling fire and swirling smoke, my ears tuned in to his words. A few moments later, my thoughts drifted in and out as he talked about following Jesus all the way.

Even though we'd connected wonderfully with a new church family, learned life-changing principles, and were overjoyed with Rick's heart response to Jesus, we hadn't given much thought to any serious church commitments.

However, something about the Sabbath intrigued me. I had questioned it for several years, wanting to know more.

My gaze toward the lake intensified as Pastor Nelson continued speaking. Then, a silent conversation between God and me commenced regarding a dilemma.

God Can Do So Much More

The issue of selling shaved ice on Saturday troubled me. The potential for this to come between *my* plans and *God's* plans was strong. He was putting it on my heart to sell the business, and I knew it. God had spoken before, and He was speaking again.

Saturday sales were most profitable, often clearing seven hundred dollars in one day after expenses and park commission. But the message from the Holy Spirit to walk away was crystal clear. Plus, I'd long given up on arguing with God. He always knew what was best.

Knowing I could produce reasonable rationales to keep the business open and operate only on weekdays, I surrendered and gave God my word to follow Him in obedience.

I don't remember everything that Pastor Nelson said, but I'll never forget the conviction coming from the Holy Spirit.

A closing appeal and prayer reclaimed my attention. After exchanging hugs with several people and thanking the pastor for his message, the thoughts began to form. *Now, what will I do? I need to decide soon.*

With that, we returned to our campsite to finish packing.

As we said goodbyes to our new friends, Rick told them, "Hey, stop by one afternoon, and we'll give you a shaved ice, on the house!"

I wish he would quit saying that, there isn't going to be any shaved ice to give away! I wanted to talk to Rick about my decision in private after we returned home and hadn't planned on him announcing free shaved ice to everyone!

He had already told at least five families the same thing when I shot him a glance followed with, "I wouldn't tell anyone else that."

My comment and strange look appeared to perplex him, but I'd hoped he'd taken my hint. The impression from God asking me to sell the business remained. And, as far as I knew, there wouldn't be any shaved ice to give away—assuming it would be sold soon.

Once again, I prayed and trusted God with the details.

We loaded up the truck and drove away with happy hearts and exhausted boys.

Much change had occurred over the weekend, and I couldn't stop praising the Lord for His goodness!

About a week before going on the campout, I'd scheduled a few days of vacation to visit my parents. After the boys hopped on the school bus Monday morning, I headed to Doddridge. Because of the rush to get on the road, I'd failed to inform Rick of my conversation with God about the Iceback Sno-Shack.

Life was good again. The strain once existing between Rick and my parents had long since evaporated. Through the months of Bible study, Mom and Dad witnessed the changes in Rick and our marriage. The relationship between all of us was much stronger! The feelings of uneasiness and discord were no longer an issue.

We certainly weren't where we wanted to be ultimately, but we were far from where we used to be! And with the recent news of Rick's response to the altar call at the campout, things were looking up!

After visiting a while longer with my parents, I prepared for bed. A few moments later, the phone rang. It was Rick.

"Are you sitting down?" he asked.

"No, do I need to? Is everything OK?" I questioned.

Before he responded, a gut feeling indicated where the conversation might go.

"A young lady from Woodlawn called a few minutes ago and wants to know if we're interested in leasing or selling our shaved-ice business." Rick paused, before continuing, "Cindy—are you there? Did you hear what I said?"

"Hmm—yes, are you serious? I mean, how did she, wait, how did you know?" I asked.

"I knew, Cindy; I could see it in your eyes Sunday morning before leaving the campground. When you commented strangely about us giving away free shaved ice, I couldn't help but wonder what was going on. I suspected God was dealing with your heart about something," he replied.

Amazing! God is working fast!

"You have *got* to be kidding me! I haven't said a word to anyone, much less advertised it!" I squealed.

No doubt, I was puzzled but readily accepted God's faithfulness and favor!

"Give me her number. I want to call her right away!" I said.

After hanging up the phone with Rick, I called her up. We agreed to meet the following Friday.

Several days later, I returned home and cleaned up the trailer for the prospective new owner. As scheduled, she arrived with her husband on Friday. After taking one look at the shaved-ice operation, she was hooked!

Without hesitation, the excited couple wrote us a check for exactly the amount we'd paid for the business less than one year prior. Rick and I stood in the driveway, shocked as we watched the Iceback Sno-Shack roll away.

Thank You, Lord, for surprising us with Your love again!

We faithfully marched on and trusted Him with our future.

Chapter 24

Rick consumed less and less alcohol, but an internal struggle remained. Although we didn't discuss it much, I knew his drinking declined because his heart was open to the Holy Spirit's conviction. He was *willing* to be changed, and he wasn't fighting as hard anymore. He genuinely wanted victory over the alcohol.

One night during our study, Rick shared a profound confession to Dave, Gary, and Dr. Samuel, "I have wonderful children, good money-making capabilities, and a beautiful wife. I had every reason in the world to do better, but I thought I needed to straighten up first, then come to Jesus. Thank you so much for sharing the little book *Steps to Christ* with me! It is leading me to scriptures in the Bible, pointing out that I *can't* straighten myself up—it's impossible. I've got to come to Jesus just the way I am."

The guys were so patient with my husband. Not once did they say, "Rick, you're going to have to quit doing this, and you need to stop doing that." Or, "Rick, we can't study the Bible with you if you drank today." God's faithful servants allowed the Holy Spirit to do the convicting and kept pointing him to Jesus week after week. They had seen for themselves Rick's genuine desire to follow Jesus as he responded to the altar call at the campout. They willingly allowed Jesus to use them as conduits contributing to Rick's spiritual growth.

A few weeks later, we studied the 2,300-day time prophecy in the Bible. Despite Dr. Samuel's wonderful detailed explanations, the lesson challenged me.

We were close to concluding the study when Rick said, "Let me see if I understand this correctly." He began reverbalizing the entire content, numbers and all, while I sat there with my mouth wide open in disbelief. *How in the world did he do that? He shouldn't be able to understand all of that heavy content in just one hour!*

Dave and Gary giggled a bit under their breath as Dr. Samuel said, smiling, "Yes sir, my friend, you got it."

Another miracle witnessed as a result of prayer, watching Rick fill his life with Jesus, who was changing him day by day, was an amazing answer to prayer! And with certainty, I could say, *He is able!*

More than able.

Exceedingly, abundantly able.

As the summer continued, Jan and Lisa encouraged us to bring the boys to a weekly meeting at church for youth called Pathfinders. The time we spent learning educational activities and spiritual content was enjoyable and fun for us all.

Not long after, we learned about a huge upcoming International Pathfinder Camporee. The other kids were pumped about the event, which, of course, fueled our boys' excitement too. Dave approached us one night and asked if we would all like to go. I didn't want to be rude, but with time away from the farm, plus the expenses of the trip, it didn't seem realistic. We agreed to talk and pray about it.

A few days later at work, Dave asked if we'd decided about the trip. Before I answered, he informed me the church would be covering all of our expenses for the trip. I couldn't believe what I was hearing. We weren't even members of the church yet!

Grateful for the generosity and the opportunity, we began making plans to go. As a bonus, the camporee dates didn't conflict with our poultry production. We were going to be out of chickens the entire week! God had worked everything out for us to go to the camporee.

We were oblivious as to what a camporee involved, but we were eager to find out.

One concern looming for me was wondering how Rick would handle his nicotine and drinking habits on the trip. We didn't discuss it, but it gnawed at me as we waited on the big day to arrive.

August 8, 2004, came quickly, and off we went with a caravan of vehicles and camping gear to Oshkosh, Wisconsin!

When we arrived, we were shocked to find thousands of tents set up and people from all over the world! Imagine our surprise when we discovered we were camping out on an aviation airfield with over thirty thousand people!

We soon realized the Adventist Church was much larger than we'd imagined, especially compared to the small church we were attending. And considering Rick was forty years old and had never heard of the Seventh-day Adventist Church, this was fairly astounding to us. Each day, the kids learned new Pathfinder honors and skills and exchanged trading pins with countless people from other countries.

The nightly, evening programming was a favorite highlight centering around the camporee theme, Faith on Fire. Thousands of people walked from their campsite to a huge field each night carrying blankets and chairs to watch the nightly drama. The very first night, two cute little girls stepped onto the stage and began to sing. Their angelic voices echoed across the sea of people and melted our hearts,

"Set my faith on fire
That's my one desire
Make my life
A pure and holy flame
So the world can see
There's a fire in me
Burning by the power
Of your name,
Start a blaze,
And set my faith . . .
. . . on fire."[1]

Immediately after the girls finished singing, my husband said, "Lord, I want You to set *my* faith on fire." A spark was lit, and we were ready to be on fire for Jesus!

The week at Oshkosh was incredible and pivotal. It was the first time Rick avoided alcohol that long in almost twenty years. I knew he'd excused himself a few times to smoke outside the campground, but I rejoiced knowing the tide was changing with his alcohol use. God was helping him one day at a time. Morning worship, wholesome fellowship, and character-enriching programs at Oshkosh built bridges for new things to come!

---

1. Mark Bond, et al., "Faith on Fire" Center for Youth Evangelism at Andrews University, 2004. Used with permission.

Chapter 25

After Oshkosh, our hearts brightly glowed with burning determination and high expectations for the future!

The mountaintop experience yielded great victories, but Rick's struggle with alcohol remained.

Since he had drunk alcohol for over twenty years of his adult life, it was safe to say the stronghold was fierce. Satan even deceived him into thinking he couldn't go to sleep without the perceived calming influence of alcohol.

Interestingly, as time went on, he noticed a stark separation from God every time he drank.

Continued convictions from the Holy Spirit grew stronger, resulting in a decreased desire for alcohol. He discovered there really was more to life than drinking all day.

We even traded out our Western movies for uplifting sermons by a pastor named Doug Batchelor. As the preacher turned toward the camera for his nightly appeal, it seemed as if he looked straight into our eyes. Often, the very subject being discussed brought conviction. Our hearts experienced transformation day by day, and we responded to God's call.

Rick developed the practice of rising early to study his Bible, then going out and doing his work. But inevitably, like clockwork, he would start drinking, and one beer turned into fifteen.

As long as he prayed, read, and studied his Bible, there was no problem. But once he walked out the door, weakness and temptation returned. One day he cried out to God with all his heart, "How am I going to do this? Because I *have* to work. I can't just read the Bible all the time."

He *knew* God heard him. Despite the frustrating, vicious cycle of torment from the enemy, Rick was certain God was drawing him to an abundant life—one that didn't include alcohol.

As he spent time in God's Word daily, the Lord led him to read Hebrews 12:1, 2, "Therefore we also, since we are surrounded by so great a cloud of witnesses, let us lay aside every weight, and the sin which so easily ensnares us, and let us run with endurance the race that is set before us, looking unto Jesus, the author and finisher of our faith, who for the joy that was set before Him endured the cross, despising the shame, and has sat down at the right hand of the throne of God."

Rick finally realized and understood for the first time that being a Christian was so much more than just going to church one day a week. Instead, God's plan included staying connected to Him 24-7.

By fixing his eyes on Jesus, Rick learned that God could give him victory over *any* besetting sin.

In the midst of his discovery, God gave him the beautiful song, "I Have Decided to Follow Jesus." He found that by singing it repeatedly, his mind stayed on Jesus—so he sang it in front of millions of chickens every day.

Another practical application he included, at the suggestion of a church member, was listening to audio sermons and the Bible while riding the tractor or repairing water and feed lines.

One Sabbath, a visiting pastor gave Rick a copy of his audio sermon, which explained that Jesus not only died on the cross to pay the price for our sin but also gave us the power to overcome sin.

Scripture memorization, especially Bible promises, became a priority. Rick filled his life with Jesus, and alcohol eventually lost its grip on him. He repeated and personalized the audio message he listened to often, "Jesus not only died to pay the price for my sin but He also died to give me the power to overcome sin!" This truth radically changed Rick's life!

One morning close to 3:00 A.M., I rolled over on my left side and noticed Rick wasn't in the bed. Panic and a sick drop in my stomach overtook me. *Surely, he isn't out drinking!*

The frightening flashbacks of the past were about to get the best of me when I suddenly detected his voice. *Who is he talking to? And what is he doing on the floor?*

God Can Do So Much More

Imagine the thrill in my soul as I discovered my husband having a conversation with God! I quietly listened to his passionate prayers and thanked my heavenly Father. *Oh Lord, You really can save to the uttermost! Thank You, Jesus!*

Routinely, the Lord began waking Rick up about 3:00 A.M. each morning. He would roll out of bed and get on his knees and say a simple prayer he meant with his whole heart, "Lord, help me. I'm in a rut."

Like me, Rick benefited from claiming Scripture promises: "And you will seek Me and find Me, when you search for Me with all your heart. I will be found by you, says the LORD, and I will bring you back from your captivity" (Jeremiah 29:13, 14).

And that's just what God was about to do!

Then one day, it finally happened. God let Rick know his fight with alcohol was over—once and for all. The entire day, he prayed and radically filled his thoughts with God's Word. And, by God's grace, the struggle ended.

When I arrived home from work that day, Rick met me in the carport, exclaiming, "Honey! I haven't had a drink *all* day long!"

Seeing and hearing this breakthrough reminded me of God's ability to do more than I could ever think or imagine!

To top it off, he went to bed that night and slept like a baby! He woke up at 3:00 A.M. again, rolled out of bed, got back on his knees, and *knew* he'd been set free! Hallelujah!

He praised and thanked God for the victory! From his heart, he recited with even more praise, Psalm 119:97–105,

"Oh, how I love Your law!
It is my meditation all the day.
You, through Your commandments, make me wiser than my enemies;
For they are ever with me.
I have more understanding than all my teachers,
For Your testimonies are my meditation.
I understand more than the ancients,
Because I keep Your precepts.
I have restrained my feet from every evil way,
That I may keep Your word.
I have not departed from Your judgments,
For You Yourself have taught me.

How sweet are Your words to my taste,
Sweeter than honey to my mouth!
Through Your precepts I get understanding;
Therefore I hate every false way.

"Your word is a lamp to my feet
And a light to my path."

In the stillness of the early morning, he joyfully acknowledged, "I've sensed the presence of God!"

The very next morning, he was amazed to discover his daily devotional reading contained the same scriptures from Psalm 119:97–105, the very ones God filled Rick's heart and mind with only hours before!

Later that morning, my husband called me at work and shared his profound experience, "Cindy, it had to be from the Holy Spirit; God lit my heart on fire for Him. I've experienced a divine encounter with Him!" he joyfully exclaimed.

Fast and simultaneously, many changes occurred. In addition to the alcohol, Rick desperately wanted to be free of his addiction to nicotine. He kept asking God to purge any additional bad habits out of his life. He was given the book *You Can Be Tobacco Free* by Kay Collins, which included special Bible promises to assist him in gaining victory. This applicable tool was added to his daily routine of praying and studying. He took one day at a time and chose to receive the grace and new mercies flowing from Jesus each day.

The process didn't happen overnight, but there were successes every single day as he chose to keep his eyes on Jesus. He tapped into every available resource offered in efforts to overcome.

Finally—drugs, lust, alcohol, cigarettes, and smokeless tobacco, in that very order, vanished as Rick crowded them all out with Jesus! These five "mountains" of sin, as Rick called them, enslaved him the majority of his adult life, and one by one, God gave him complete victory!

The following month, we attended an Amazing Facts Bible prophecy seminar at the church, presented by Tyler Long. The nightly series of meetings solidified the principles we'd learned from the beginning of our Thursday-night Bible studies with Dave.

Serious conversations between Rick and me regarding our commitment to

Jesus began. We wanted to honor Him for His faithfulness!

We sat and listened to each seminar presentation, basking in awe of how many miracles God had manifested in our lives. We suspected there was more to come.

About midway through the seminar, we said to each other, "If we're going to do this Christian thing, then let's do it all the way."

Decision made, we were going to follow Jesus wholeheartedly—forward, on our knees. The rest of our lives belonged to Him, and we wanted Jesus right in the center.

Chapter 26

We eagerly went forward with our new commitment to follow Jesus, but one item remained on the table—money.

Although my husband sent a little cash here and there for offering, and was OK with me tithing and giving offerings from the nursing income, he never felt compelled or convicted to tithe or give offerings to God from farm income.

But now, we'd made the commitment to trust God 100 percent. Not wanting to push, I prayed—letting God do the convicting.

Not long after, Rick said, "It's time. I want to start returning tithe and giving offerings from the farm income. I don't want to hold anything back from God anymore."

We had just gone all in with God when a *big* temptation came.

One evening, a good friend of ours stopped by for a visit. He and Rick were sitting on the tailgate of his truck when, moments later, a feed truck pulled into the driveway en route to the chicken houses.

The truck came to a slow roll, and about that time, our friend pointed to the driver and said, "Hey, that's one of my former employees." The driver also recognized our friend about the same time and stopped the truck. He hopped out and began to chitchat with our friend. My husband was familiar with many of the feed-truck drivers, except this one.

Our friend looked at my husband and then directed his attention toward his former employee and said, "Hey, why don't you hook my buddy Rick up with some extra feed?"

The driver looked at my husband, nodded, and replied directly to him, "Sure, I can do that. I don't have the extra feed on my truck today, just your normal load, but next time I'm here, I'll take care of you. Just slip me a twenty-dollar bill each time, and we'll call it good."

"Oh, man! That would be great!" my husband replied excitedly.

The driver climbed up into his truck, drove down to the poultry houses, and proceeded to fill up the empty feed bins.

"Wait! I can't believe I just agreed to that. Go tell your friend to forget this conversation ever happened. And, tell him I don't want to ever see him here again. I just gave my farm to the Lord, and the enemy just tempted me to do something very wrong," my husband said intently. And with that, our friend did as Rick requested, and the conversation was over.

No doubt, the extra helping of feed would've really boosted our profit margin since poultry feed was our biggest expense on the farm.

Unfortunately, about the same time, we contracted a terrible disease on our poultry farm called gangrene dermatitis. This illness resulted in the loss of about one thousand four-pound birds by the time we reached the end of the grow-out period.

In order for the birds to attain the desired maturity weight, they needed approximately eight pounds of feed. And once the one thousand birds died, it was like throwing away eight thousand pounds of feed—wasted and gone. Unfortunately, the disastrous cycle peaked the last seven days over several grow-outs, resulting in a devastating loss of income.

We had exhausted all of our resources in an attempt to eradicate the disease, being told controlling the problem was the best we could hope for. Our contracting poultry company offered little assistance, only adding to our mounting frustrations.

This temptation dangled in Rick's face was real. The extra feed could've made a tremendous difference, making up for thousands of lost dollars because of the disease on our farm.

Despite the challenges and enemy enticements, God quickly rewarded Rick for his faithfulness to trust Him. The very next grow-out, Rick was informed about a product that could supposedly suppress the disease.

My husband and father-in-law, Sam, decided it was worth a try, so they traveled four hours to pick up the suggested treatment. On the way there, my husband saw a church sign: "It's time to stop worrying and start praying."

He knew God was speaking this message to him. So that's exactly what he did—prayed and trusted God.

When they arrived at the business to pick up the recommended treatment, Sam engaged in a conversation with a poultry technician inside the store while Rick loaded the truck and trailer with the litter treatment. The gentleman told my father-in-law, "It's OK to get the litter treatment, but it won't help that much. I'll tell you how to get rid of the disease with some practical, cost-friendly suggestions."

They drove away with six-thousand pounds of litter treatment anyway, plus the hopeful, helpful tips.

Almost immediately by the next grow-out, the disease was completely gone, and we made ten thousand dollars more than the grow-out before. God blessed in a powerful way! Normally, we produced seven grow-outs per year, so the potential of having an increase of seventy thousand dollars per year was a great possibility.

We were overwhelmed with the miraculous turnaround and sensed God's favor in a huge way, encouraging us to trust Him even more. We recalled His promise:

> "Bring all the tithes into the storehouse,
> That there may be food in My house,
> And try Me now in this,"
> Says the Lord of hosts,
> "If I will not open for you the windows of heaven
> And pour out for you such blessing
> That there will not be room enough to receive it" (Malachi 3:10).

When we'd made the total-commitment decision, it meant *everything*—our hearts, business, desires, talents, motives, and money belonged to Him.

Now, it seemed our decision to go all in with Jesus was complete, except for one more thing.

Chapter 27

One night, Rick and I sat at home talking together. The Bible-prophecy seminar neared completion, and we felt drawn to join the Seventh-day Adventist Church—a movement of believers who valued the Bible as the authoritative Word of God.

With our hearts in perfect agreement about taking this step, we knelt together. A deep and holy peace filled the room as I listened to my husband's quiet prayer sealing our commitment to give full allegiance to the King of kings.

We could hardly wait to share our decision with Dave, Gary, Dr. Samuel, and all the others who had so lovingly mentored and nurtured our walk with Christ!

The next night at the seminar, Rick and I sat hand in hand listening to Pastor Long's message. He closed by urging the congregation to follow Jesus all the way.

Rick and I glanced at each other, smiling. We wanted to jump up right then and share our good news!

Pastor Long invited everyone to sing, "Turn Your Eyes Upon Jesus" and then closed with prayer. He walked to the back of the sanctuary to shake hands and answer questions, but we didn't follow.

Instead, we quickly motioned for Dave, Gary, and Dr. Samuel to join us at our seats. Several other members were standing near us as well.

Rick grinned and announced, "Cindy and I are so happy—as if you couldn't tell. We want to spend the rest of our lives serving Jesus, and we believe this is where God wants us to be. We are ready to respond to His call and follow Him all the way. We want to be baptized and make Him Lord of our lives forever!"

Hearing Rick say these words almost took my breath away! The response around us was immediate.

Within seconds, Dave and Rick were sharing a hug.

Simultaneously, "Hallelujah!" and "Amen!" broke out from Gary, Dr. Samuel, and others. The scene of rejoicing was priceless.

Seeing the expression on Dave's face—the tears rolling down his cheeks—said it all. Everyone knew he had prayed and labored for this moment a long, long while.

Moments later, Jan, Lisa, Pastor Long, and his wife, Lavonne, all joined us in the sacred moment of celebration. Many hugs and much excitement filled the air!

A feeling of sheer bliss overtook me as I looked around. These dear friends were about to become our church family. Delight filled my heart as I realized how special everyone was to us.

We set our baptism date—November 6, 2004—and joyously began inviting friends and family!

My dad, who'd witnessed the undisputed transformation in Rick through the months, now extended his sense of cautious protection to both of us. Wanting to be supportive of our decision, but also careful, he asked, "Are you sure you know what you're doing?"

Without hesitation, we replied, "We've never been more certain about anything in our entire lives!"

I often marveled at how clearly everyone around us could see that God had changed our home and marriage "exceeding abundantly."

Rick was on fire for the Lord! His transformation reminded me of how Saul of Tarsus became the mighty apostle Paul when he encountered the risen Lord on the Road to Damascus. Every day, I saw a new Rick—filled with love for God and me.

Over the months of studying together, the Savior miraculously restored our hearts toward each other, and my husband was now my best friend, my protector, and my rock.

The crisp fall Sabbath morning of our commitment celebration arrived. Driving into the church parking lot, we noticed people carrying food into the fellowship hall for the afternoon lunch. They waved in welcome as we parked the car, and I couldn't stop smiling.

Brooks, Farron, Tyler, and Reece walked into church with us, watching in awe as we were greeted at the door with beautiful corsages. Entering the sanctuary, I felt both a solemn peace and great anticipation.

Rick and I are walking into a new chapter of our life with You, God! This is really happening!

I slipped to the back to put our items in the changing room behind the baptistry, pausing briefly to listen to the water gently swirling. I heard the pianist begin playing "Great Is Thy Faithfulness," and the beautifully blended sounds of water and piano lit yet another flame in my heart!

Looking over the glass partition at the warm water, I trailed my fingers through the rose petals that floated on top. *I can't wait to step in the water! This is so wonderful!*

Glancing up, I saw the wooden cross hanging above the baptistry, draped in white.

A lump formed in my throat as I flashed back in memory to several months earlier when we'd sat around our dining room table visiting with Dave and Gary after a Bible study. Gary, who did beautiful woodwork, mentioned he was making a cross for the sanctuary.

Rick immediately retrieved three large spiked nails from his antique collection and gave them to Gary. Now I saw those iron spikes hammered in where the hands and feet of Jesus were nailed for our salvation.

Under this cross, Rick and I would be buried in Christ and rise to new life in Him.

Thank You, Lord, for Your love. Thank You for this amazing day and the people who have made us feel so special!

Back in the sanctuary again, I noticed our boys leading song service with the other kids. In the foyer, Rick welcomed our parents. Soon his brother

161

Mark slipped in—then Mack and Donna with our niece and nephew.

A host of other friends and coworkers followed not far behind. I knew Kristi and Karen both had prior commitments, but they had each called us earlier to share their happiness and congratulations.

The lump in my throat grew. How amazing to see these faces who'd been with us from the beginning. The entire journey, spanning from our first blind date all the way to our baptism, was nothing short of a modern-day miracle!

After the morning lesson study, Rick and I donned our pristine white baptismal robes and sat on the front row. Pastor Ross spoke a few words, then invited us to stand and share our testimony. Tears welled in our eyes as we thanked everyone for their love and encouragement.

Next, Dave took the microphone. With deep emotion, he shared how God put the call in his heart to reach out to Rick over a year before. As I listened to him affirm God's leading in our lives, I remembered his compassion and faithfulness through all those long months of study.

Pastor Ross then asked us a series of questions related to the baptism, and we triumphantly declared our commitment to follow Jesus the rest of our lives!

We walked to the baptistry, and Dave and Pastor Ross entered the water first. I could barely contain my composure as Dave assisted me down the steps.

Rick followed behind and took my hand as he reached my side. Looking into my husband's eyes, I felt engulfed by the love and awe reflected in his warm smile.

Together we were buried with Christ.

Together we arose to an abundant new life in God.

Pastor Ross prayed, and the four of us tearfully embraced.

Finally, we turned together and faced the congregation while they welcomed Rick and Cindy Mercer as the newest members of the Pine Bluff Seventh-day Adventist Church.

At home that evening, we enjoyed a meal with our parents and boys, basking in the afterglow of the day's events. Hearing our family share their favorite moments of the day brought extra joy—their happiness for us thrilled our hearts.

Before going to bed, we continued a priceless principle we'd learned from Lisa and gathered together for family worship.

God Can Do So Much More

Later, while drifting off to sleep, I wondered what the years ahead would bring. *What do You have in store for us next, God?*

I still remembered the remaining part of His promise to me on that long-ago morning in the bathroom. He had said He would use Rick in ministry.

I don't yet know how this will happen, God—but I can't wait to find out!

Chapter 28

Rick and I were on top of the world after our baptism! Our hearts rejoiced in all the brand-new possibilities of our brand-new life, and we wanted to share Jesus with anyone who would listen!

Church members encouraged us by saying, "When you're willing to be used by God, there are no limits to what He will do with you!"

We now stood on solid ground with our hope anchored in Jesus and learned to lean on His precious promises more than ever! We knew we were no match for Satan and his fiery darts, so we guarded our hearts closely with the Word.

Isaiah 40:28, 29 delivered assurance right on time.

> Have you not known?
> Have you not heard?
> The everlasting God, the LORD,
> The Creator of the ends of the earth,
> Neither faints nor is weary.
> His understanding is unsearchable.
> He gives power to the weak,
> And to those who have no might He increases strength.

These beautiful words in Isaiah not only applied to God's abundant blessings, but they also became a tower of strength in our times of greatest tragedy—when we faced one of our starkest losses with no answers, only pain.

Two weeks after our baptism, Rick and I looked forward to an early Thanksgiving with my parents. What a perfect way to continue the joy of our life-changing celebration!

On my last day at work before the holiday, Dave and I chatted between surgery cases. He, Lisa, and the boys planned to leave the next day to visit her family in Colorado.

After taking the last patient to the recovery room, we made a sprinting dash for the locker room. Within minutes, we were back in the hallway at the same time, exchanging quick goodbyes as we hurried toward the door.

Dave dashed out toward the parking lot with his ball cap in his hands only to turn back seconds later, with a special smile on his face.

"Cindy, I want to say again how excited I am! God is doing amazing things in you and Rick! I can't see Him leaving Rick as a chicken farmer—He has big plans! Well, see you soon. Enjoy your time with your family!" When he finished, a big grin formed as he socked his ball cap on his head and ran out again.

"Have a great Thanksgiving," I called after him as the door closed behind him.

That was the last time I saw our dear friend and spiritual mentor, Dave. The very next day, a tragic automobile accident in Clayton, New Mexico, claimed Lisa's life and left Dave with serious head injuries. After a med-flight to an Amarillo, Texas, hospital, he remained in critical condition.

Rick and I joined our church family in constant prayer. We desperately wanted to be there for him, but he seemed to be a world away from us.

Dave's witness to us was priceless, and now we stood helplessly by, unable to do anything. The stress mounted as days rolled on.

For five days, we prayed and waited, hoping for good news to come. Instead, the updates were grim. On Thanksgiving morning, we received the hard news that our buddy Dave was asleep in Jesus.

Our heartache was unbearable. We could hardly imagine the thought of not having Dave and Lisa in our life anymore.

Although their sons, Jake and Jordan, survived the accident with minimal injuries, our hearts broke at their unspeakable loss. Soon after Dave and Lisa's celebration of life service, the boys transitioned to the loving home of imme-diate family in another state.

With the tragedy still fresh, I feared Rick might slip back into his old hab-its. But God didn't let that happen. By divine design, He placed us in a small, loving church family who were poised and ready to involve Rick in service. We began leading out in Bible studies with others, including some Dave had started before the accident.

The small church offered and encouraged leadership and growth opportu-nities, which helped Rick and me thrive in service for the Lord!

In less than one year, Rick was ordained as an elder and began receiving in-vitations almost every Sabbath to share a message at one of the three churches in the district.

God opened door after door, and we willingly followed every time.

One morning, Rick and I arrived at the Three Angels Broadcasting Net-work in Illinois to share our testimony to a worldwide audience on the *3ABN Today* show. As I stood looking into the mirror in preparation for the inter-view, God again requested my attention.

Joy filled my eyes as He turned my thoughts back to the day He'd first promised to give me a testimony. Now, He was allowing me to share His faithfulness with the whole world!

More tears built up as I looked deep into Rick's eyes, "Honey, this is more than I ever could've imagined! Four years ago, I gazed into *our* bathroom mirror during one of my lowest points ever. There was no hope for our mar-riage. We were close to becoming another divorce statistic—a casualty from the enemy. But look! Here we are about to share the amazing miracle God performed in our life! Not only did God give me the promised testimony, but He also is about to let me share it with the whole world via satellite TV programming! God is *so* good!"

"Cindy, I don't know where I'd be if you hadn't prayed and trusted God. He saved me and restored our relationship and marriage!" Rick exclaimed.

We hugged and praised God for His faithfulness and mercy!

As the months passed, Rick and I couldn't deny the overwhelming sense that God was calling *us* into full-time ministry. The more we talked and prayed, the more excited we became. But we felt unsure about how this might develop. We were willing to do anything that God wanted us to do, including evangelism, overseas missions, or Bible work.

One day, Rick shared with his mom that we both felt drawn to enter some form of Christian service.

She immediately responded, "If God wants you in the ministry, He'll provide someone to buy your farm."

That *very* evening, I overheard Rick on the phone saying, "Really, you're interested in buying our farm?" My jaw dropped as I walked closer to him.

We haven't even advertised the farm for sale, Lord! You are amazing!

"Sounds great, I'll get with you tomorrow," he continued.

Rick beamed as he hung up the phone!

"Can you believe this? God is working fast, Cindy!"

This was nothing short of a miraculous, magnificent faith booster! We squealed with excitement as we embraced and once again gave thanks to the Lord!

We were confident God would work out the details. He had done it before, and we knew He would do it again! Negotiations were soon underway, and the unimaginable process of selling our farm became a reality!

Walking out of the lawyer's office after our property closing, Rick experienced a sobering jolt.

For the first time in his adult life, his income-making capabilities were no longer his security. He had already let his CPA license expire, and now with the poultry farm gone, God was his only security—there was no turning back!

We were well aware after signing on the dotted line that our financial portfolio would never be the same. We weren't worried because our faith was in Jesus, and selling the farm was a joyous answer to prayer!

But that didn't stop the enemy from invoking doubt at this crucial intersection in our lives. *You're going to serve God in ministry? Ha, ha! You have a horrible past, what makes you think anyone would allow* you *to work in ministry? You don't even have a theology degree!*

The likelihood of any conference hiring Rick was slim at best. But we hung on to the assurance that the One who'd arranged the sale of the farm also held our future securely in His hand. Resolutely, we tuned out the jeering doubts and waited for God to guide—just as He had promised.

One night, Rick told me he'd been impressed to ask Pastor Ross how he could help him out while we listened to see where God would lead us next.

"He didn't even hesitate," Rick reported. "He just told me, visit, visit, visit."

Pray Big

Rick became Pastor Ross's volunteer assistant, doing anything necessary to help. He kept our truck wheels rolling and the odometer climbing as he prayerfully covered the large district territory.

He preached at the three churches, gave Bible studies, and even joined the pastor at funeral services. Several months passed with Rick volunteering, serving with all his heart—and receiving outstanding on-the-job training.

One day, while volunteering at the Benton church food pantry, Rick's cell phone rang. He answered and immediately recognized the voice.

"Rick, I've heard you're on fire for Jesus! Would you be interested in pastoring two churches in southern Arkansas?" It was Elder Steve Orian, our Arkansas-Louisiana Conference president.

Rick told me after the call ended from Elder Orian that all he heard were thousands of angels singing in his ears the song, "Great Is Thy Faithfulness!"

Immediately we knew that a gateway for formal ministry had opened. We enthusiastically stepped through the threshold of a beautiful new beginning; confident God would equip us for the assignment ahead.

The Magnolia and El Dorado church district warmly welcomed us and became like close family within a short period of time. Little did we know, God was preparing us for something even more!

After two wonderful years of faithful service in Southern Arkansas, we were presented an opportunity to serve in full-time ministry! The bittersweet moment arrived as we said our goodbyes and made our way to a land of tumbleweeds, sandburs, and stunning sunsets!

The Oklahoma Panhandle seemed so far away from "home," but our excited church family welcomed us with open arms, easing the transition.

One late November, only months after arriving at our new hometown of Woodward, Rick received a phone call from the Shattuck church head elder as he finished a hospital visit.

"Hey, Pastor Rick, this is Wayne. I need your prayers. My dad isn't doing well. He's in the hospital with a brain aneurysm," Wayne solemnly said.

"I'm so sorry. Where is he, Wayne?" Rick asked.

"Amarillo, Texas," replied Wayne.

We lived almost three hours from Amarillo, but without hesitating, Rick said, "I'm on my way."

He left the hospital parking lot immediately and drove straight there.

After arriving, he hurriedly marched toward the emergency room trauma entrance. He was steps away from the building when God stopped him.

"Look where you are, Rick. You are a pastor now. You're about to minister to a family in the very same hospital where Dave took his last breath."

All Rick could say was, "Oh God, You are so faithful!"

Rick pondered the irony of it all. Only four years earlier, to the very month, Dave struggled for his life in the very same trauma center. The distance between Amarillo and Southeast Arkansas seemed eons away at the time of the accident. Yet, God brought my husband full circle to Amarillo for a family now in need.

Rick's heart raced as he realized God performed another miracle—a personal confirmation He'd called him into ministry. Rick knew he was right where God wanted him to be, doing exactly what He wanted him to do.

Dave often spoke eagerly of standing on the sea of glass one day. I can still see him sitting at our dining room table throughout all our months of study. His eyes would light up with anticipation each time he vividly described how he pictured eternity.

Today, Rick and I often speak of the triumphant moment when we will meet Dave and Lisa again. Rick says when he gets to heaven, he's first going to hug Jesus, and then he's going to run up to Dave on the sea of glass and give him the biggest hug ever.

What a moment that will be! Dave has *no idea* Rick became a pastor!

The last time Dave saw Rick, he was a newly baptized prosperous chicken farmer with a converted heart. Because Dave heard the Holy Spirit's call to reach out and suggest Bible studies, God used his faithful obedience as the catalyst leading to Rick's salvation.

I can picture Jesus standing on the sea of glass with the two of them—lovingly showing them the full scope of His amazing plan.

I can picture Jesus drawing their attention to a large crowd nearby—men, women, and children also standing on the sea of glass because of God's ministry through Rick and me.

Each joyous face will be a story of deliverance—addictions conquered, marriages restored, depression lifted, spiritual renewals, and revivals in individual hearts shared with our dear friends on that glad reunion day!

Even so, come, Lord Jesus!

For over twelve years, God has given us the privilege to serve in pastoral and prayer ministry.

After our time in Arkansas and Oklahoma, He brought us to the beautiful Blue Ridge Mountains in the Carolina Conference. Recently, God moved us yet again—bringing us home to pastor in Arkansas.

Sometimes, in the middle of our busy weeks overflowing with church appointments, prayer meetings, evangelistic seminars, fall roundup, and so much more, I look back to what I wrote in my journal on the night of my first blind date with Rick:

Thank You, God, for sending him to me—I promise You, we will serve You forever.

On that night long ago, as I envisioned my grand life story, I couldn't begin to imagine what lay ahead for Rick, me, our family, and our ministry—but God knew!

He saw something far beyond anything we could see!

"For My thoughts are not your thoughts,
Nor are your ways My ways," says the LORD.
"For as the heavens are higher than the earth,
So are My ways higher than your ways,
And My thoughts than your thoughts" (Isaiah 55:8, 9).

When God spoke to me that early morning in the bathroom years ago, everything seemed lost. But He told me, *"Cindy, if you leave, you will not have a testimony—I want to use your husband in the ministry,"* and I believed Him.

I still believe Him with my whole heart—and my faith has only grown stronger by His grace. Trusting Him to fulfill His promise still requires daily time with Him and the obedience to take daily steps of faith whenever I hear His voice.

But the testimony He promised that day continues growing stronger. I share it everywhere He sends me:

- Wrestle and stay in the ring.
- Clamor for the crumbs falling from the Master's table.
- Crawl through a crowded street to touch the hem of His garment.

God Can Do So Much More

- Pray, and keep on praying, through the fog.
- Wear God out with your prayers!
- Do whatever you have to do—but *never* give up on God!

Jesus *has more,* so much more than you can ever think or imagine! "Now to Him who is able to do exceedingly abundantly above all that we ask or think, according to the power that works in us" (Ephesians 3:20).

You can contact the Mercers at www.mercerministries.com.

Find, like, follow, and message us on Facebook or Instagram: Mercer Ministries.

Thank You

Although I'd love to mention a million names here, I'll have to limit myself to a few that deserve honorable mention. The following individuals and groups have poured out unlimited love, support, and prayers consistently throughout the book-writing process. Words seem inadequate to describe my appreciation, but I'm going to make a good effort here to convey my thanks!

To my precious husband, Rick—You are the best coach, companion, friend, and mate in ministry ever! Thank you for encouraging and praying for me every time you saw me with my head in my hands at the computer. All of the meals you cooked, house-cleaning duties you took on, and the many phone calls you fielded during the writing process *never* went unnoticed. When you told me years ago, "I promise I'll make you the best husband ever," I know you meant it with all your heart. You've fulfilled that promise a million times over! Your love and devotion for me and God captivates my heart. Hold on—the best is yet to come! Thank you for saying yes to Jesus, which eternally changed everything! Our life together is far more than anything I ever imagined. I love you so much!

Mom and Dad—My life is richly blessed by your endless support and love for me. You know me better than most—and you still love me! Thank you for responding encouragingly to every text or phone call when I needed your advice and opinions as the story was written. I'm forever grateful God chose you to be my parents!

Farron, Brooks, Tyler, and Reece—How in the world did I get so blessed to have such wonderful boys? This journey wasn't easy—but God restored our family and blessed us tenfold. Your many prayers and support sustained me. I'll always love you more!

Mack, Donna, Mark, Sam, and Brenda—Although I know many parts of this story were difficult to read and the road wasn't always easy, I want to thank you for always loving me and hanging in there. God was up to something even when we couldn't see it. Praise God for what He has done in our lives! I love you all so much!

Kelly Mowrer—God brought you into my life and revealed to me that you were the one to help me shape my words into written form for this book. I'm certain you didn't know what you were getting into with me when I asked you to help, but I'm so thankful that you didn't run the other way! I praise God for your intuition and candid advice, not to mention the countless hours spent at the computer and on the phone dialoging with me day after day. You invested your heart and the dividends will be witnessed for eternity. *Thank you* just doesn't seem adequate to describe my gratitude for the time you invested. You took the journey with me and we made it by God's grace to the finish line. Thanks for being my big sister, I'll love you forever!

Pastor Ross Harris and Pine Bluff, Arkansas, Seventh-day Adventist church—You took us in and loved, discipled, and nurtured us and showed us what Jesus looks like through your commitment and sacrifice. Thank you, Gary and Dr. Samuel, for the many hours of Bible study and prayers. Thank you for not giving up on us! We love you so much! Jan, thank you for your weekly sacrifice while Gary was gone for hours telling Rick, "It's all about Jesus!"

Jerry and Janet Page—I'm not sure I would've made it this far without your continual prayers and counsel. Thank you for believing in me and rooting me on when the rough days arose. I'll never forget your prayerful hearts and vision for helping me make it to the finish line! When many decisions needed to be made, your honesty and spiritual depth radiated to help me make the best choice. Thanks for taking this journey with me!

Ruthie and Don Jacobsen—Thank you for taking a chance on us "kids" many years ago! You both have a special place in our heart that grows each day. We've said a lot of prayers together and suspect we will keep doing so until Jesus comes back! We love you dearly.

James Black—Thank you for partnering with me in prayer and supporting me at just the right moments. I can't thank you enough for your powerful prayers and ability to help me see God's plan to go boldly forward in His Name. It is an honor to serve the Lord with you!

Dr. Philip Samaan—God brought us together through unusual circumstances that I'm convinced were a heavenly arrangement. Your deep, heartfelt prayers and counsel have been a tremendous blessing! Our friendship is near and dear to my heart.

Dr. Ron and Lisa Clouzet—Your timely, candid feedback and valuable input were providential during the writing process. The prayers and friendship over the years are super special to Rick and me. Thank you so much for your valuable time!

Donna Jackson—Your kindness and encouragement throughout the years are priceless. I'm privileged to call you friend. Please know your prayers have truly made a difference.

Karen Drexler—You have been a rock and true friend! You always listened, never pushed, and patiently prayed through some difficult times. It is amazing how God brought us together at such a perfect time. *Thank you* just doesn't seem to be enough. Love you much!

Mid-Central US and Carolina Conference Prayer Teams—You will never know how much your relentless prayers have meant to me! You held my hands up high when my strength failed me. I'm blessed beyond measure for your sacrificial prayers.

Gail Coridan and Marian Parson—I pestered you so much with urgent prayer requests. You never failed me once! Thank you both for being my "extra moms!"

Bryan Yeagley—You are a trooper! Wow—it is over! I can't thank you enough for laboring over my manuscript on your Hawaiian vacation, as well as your timely editing skills and input on everything from A to Z. I'm really sorry for the late-night texts, emails, and phone calls—really. Now on to the next book!

Melody Mason—You are a blessing! I love how we carried our "babies" (our books) into the delivery room together! You have been a tremendous blessing and encourager and I'll never forget it. Maybe the text messages will slow down for a little while. Our Arkansas hearts have bonded even more over this last year—I love you so much! I truly treasure our friendship.

Dottie Theriault—Your confirmation that time was of the essence in writing this book will never be forgotten. I love your servant's heart and I'm forever grateful! Your special blessing to us will *never* be forgotten!

Becky Carpenter—You win the gold medal for your patience with me on the book cover—somehow, we got it done! Thank you for hanging in there.

Dixie Strong, Ann-Marie Bates, Robin Davis, Crystal Earnhardt, Joan Mobley, Barbara LaFave, Ashley Gibbs, Kristen Cook, and Carol Marsden: Thank you for your daily prayers for my children and this book. Heaven will be amazing as we see the many answers to our many prayers from our prayer group through the years!

Elder Steve Orian—I'll never forget how you extended Rick a call into ministry many years ago. Clearly, it was a risk. But it was a risk you took for Jesus. We are honored and eternally grateful!

Arkansas State Board of Nursing—I couldn't say it then, but I can say it now. Thank you for not reinstating my nursing license upon moving back to Arkansas. It gave me time to write the book!

To all our church family, present and past—Thank you for loving us like family and taking this journey with us. You have marked a special spot on our hearts that words can't describe!

To countless family, friends, and acquaintances from all over the world—You had a huge part to play in the completion of the book. Your calls, texts, emails, cards, and Facebook posts were innumerable. Many of you held my feet to the fire for which I'm glad now! I'll never forget you cheering me on to the finish line!

To the reader—Thank you for investing your time and taking this journey with me. Never doubt God always has something more for you—so much more! Believe Him with all of your heart.

Pray Big

To the memory of Dave and Lisa Voth,
Their sacrifice and perseverance to reach one more for
the kingdom will never be forgotten!
One day very soon, the joyful celebration and reunion will
commence on the sea of glass. Hallelujah, we are one day closer!